For John
with Best wishes!

THE ONLY
HOME
THEY KNEW

Aberlour Orphanage
& WW1 Memories

Anne Black

Anne Black

ISBN 978-1-9999251-0-9

Designed and Published by MDPD
(enquiries@mdpd.co.uk)

Acknowledgements

I am very grateful to many people for their support while I was collating WW1 letters and diary events from Aberlour Orphanage to produce "The Only Home They Knew".

This book has been enhanced by excellent photos relevant to WW1 and to Aberlour Orphanage.

The photos have been obtained from Aberlour Child Care Trust Archives, National Library of Scotland WW1 collections and the Scottish Military Research Group.

Each photo is credited to the appropriate source.

I am very grateful to these organisations for agreeing to the inclusion of their photos in this book.

Family and friends have been very important to me while writing this book and have encouraged me to continue even when the task seemed overwhelming.

Special thanks to Alison Masson who proof read an early draft of the book.

David and Sandra from MDPD have provided support, guidance, professionalism and been endlessly patient and their work has been much appreciated.

To Aberlour Child Care Trust thank you for the excellent archives and for access to them. Many of the writers feel like family after years of reading their honest and moving letters.

Anne Black

Photo from National Library of Scotland's WW1 Collections.

Events and publications to commemorate the years of WW1 have been many and varied with different perspectives about the War from a wide range of organisations and people.

Some publications review the historical events of WW1 and new insights emerge along with personal testimonies that have been gathered by organisations and families.

This commemorative book which has been collated from Aberlour Child Care Trust's archives is, we feel, different from many others.

It records the events of the war through the eyes of one large "family", a family with nearly 300 "sons" at the Front. It records the experiences, perceptions and feelings of "old boys" at the Front as well as chronicling the activities, joys, fears, struggles and sadness of the "family" in Scotland waiting anxiously for the war to end.

The large family was the Aberlour Orphanage on Speyside in the North of Scotland.

Aberlour Orphanage over the years

Aberlour Orphanage was built in the late 1870s in the village of Charleston of Aberlour on Speyside.

It was founded with money given to Canon Jupp, a priest of the Episcopal Church, by a local landowner, Miss MacPherson Grant. She had asked Canon Jupp to become her private Chaplain, a post he only accepted after he convinced her to agree that a church, home and school all ought to be built on the given ground. Canon Jupp had seen first-hand in the North of England the poverty and suffering of many children whose parents had died or had been unable to provide them with a home because they had no house, work or money. His mission was to make children's lives better and give them a loving home.

Canon Jupp started his long career in caring for children with four "mitherless bairns" in a cottage by the burn of the Lour in Aberlour in 1876.

The sudden death of his benefactor Miss MacPherson Grant in 1877 created many problems. The resourceful Canon Jupp determined that he would continue the work started. Through seeking out donations and legacies and making appeals to church congregations across the country to provide funds for the Orphanage, he achieved his first goal of a small home and school.

This was made possible by a generous donation from a local landowner and with the monies Canon Jupp had collected, the Orphanage expanded initially to provide accommodation for 25 children. By the start of World War 1 about 500 children were living in the Orphanage. Over the years till the Orphanage closed in 1967 it provided a home to well over 6000 children.

Photo from Aberlour Child Care Trust Archives.

Canon Jupp believed that a good education was integral to the Orphanage as well as providing a farm and gardens where lads were trained for working on the land. For the older girls, domestic training was provided to fit them for posts in the large houses around Aberlour.

St Margaret's Episcopal Church was the Orphanage Church and services were held daily as well as several on Sundays. The beautiful building was completed in 1879 and was consecrated on November 29th 1879.

The founder Canon Jupp died in 1911 and he was succeeded by Canon Jenks who was the Warden throughout the years of WW1.

During the early 1960s, the Orphanage gradually developed smaller homes across the North of Scotland and by 1967 all the children had moved from the Orphanage and the buildings were closed and were sold.

The Aberlour Child Care Trust still continues to provide extensive services which offer imaginative and skilled care and support to children and families across Scotland.

Letters and The Aberlour Orphanage Magazine

When war started in August 1914, many "old boys" did not hesitate to join up and over the period of the War around 300 boys were serving in the Forces across the various theatres of War.

Many of the "old boys" wrote letters through those war years to the only home they knew, Aberlour Orphanage. Some of these letters were transcribed and published each month in the Aberlour Orphanage Magazine.

The Journal was a vehicle for seeking funds and material goods from the wider public and for thanking Aberlour supporters for their generosity in helping the Orphanage to survive in the War years and beyond. The extracts give glimpses of Orphanage life during the war, the struggles to make ends meet, the sorrow when an old boy was missing or was confirmed to have died and the joy when news came of the survival of any of the boys.

Sadly, many of the letter writers died during the War and their names are among those inscribed on the simple granite cross which stands outside St Margaret's Church.

In this book, the commitment of the Orphanage and staff to the boys during the war and the welcome home for those who returned during the war and at the end of hostilities is well documented.

There were Aberlour supporters across the UK who sent letters and parcels to the boys at the Front and several of the letters from the boys acknowledge the importance of being remembered by so many. Tins of cocoa, socks and fruit cake seem to have been the favourite gifts- many shared their edible gifts with others in their battalions as Orphanage boys looked out for others even in the trenches and in horrible conditions. One letter records that some of the Aberlour boys gave all their parcels to Russian Prisoners of War as they saw them starving and having no contact with family or friends.

Front: L-R Canon Charles Jupp, Mr John White. Rear: Canon Walter Jenks.

Key Aberlour characters

One of the key characters mentioned in the letters is Canon Jenks who took over as Warden of Aberlour on the death of Canon Jupp, the founder, in 1911.

Canon Jenks was often seen as an austere man but his notes in the journals show the depth of his feelings and his sadness at hearing of the death of any old boy. He latterly questioned the point of war, worried about the sense of duty that Aberlour had instilled into the boys and the sacrifices of so many of the Aberlour family.

Other staff who were frequently mentioned included Mr John White- he was an Orphanage boy himself but he stayed on as a worker and took a special pride in the gardens. Many boys refer to the Botany lessons he gave them and he became a world- renowned begonia expert as well as selling bulbs across the UK. His begonias were singled out for praise at a Paris Flower show in 1915.

Mr White went on to be Treasurer and sub Warden and his commitment to Aberlour was lifelong.

Mr Robinson was the inspiration behind many of the musical performances and plays at the Orphanage and several letters refer to various musical productions across the years.

Mr Kissack was the deputy Headmaster and it may have been he who collated the information for the Journal along with the Warden.

Miss Findlay is mentioned frequently in the letters and she sent many, many letters and parcels to the boys at the Front. She was probably the lady who sent the fruit cakes which were much appreciated. She is likely to have been a local staunch supporter of Aberlour along with many others mentioned in the monthly journal from Aberlour.

Many old boys referred in their letters to the Jupp Sales which took place twice a year at the Orphanage. Most boys expressed their disappointment that they were not to be at their "usual" stall to help. People came from across the North of Scotland to these twice-yearly Sales and it was recorded that busloads of people arrived hours before the Sale opened.

The main articles for sale were clothes, shoes and bedding.

In 1885 Canon Jupp contended that Aberlour had invented the Jumble Sale!

The money raised at these Sales to care for the "orphans" was a source of considerable income to the Orphanage. Some Sales made around £300 which when recalculated at today's value would be no less than £12,000!

Of the 300 young men who fought in WW1, the records show that at the end of the war 167 were unwounded, 58 were wounded, 62 killed in action, 5 were Prisoners of War and 9 remained listed as missing. It is likely that many more old boys died but their deaths were not reported to the Orphanage. The boys all refer to Aberlour as the "old home" and have many happy memories that they recall while they are facing daily danger, fear and pain as they fought in Europe and beyond.

Almost every letter from an old boy expressed the hope that he will be "spared" to see the "old home" again.

What also shines through is the pride the old boys showed in the courage and sacrifices of their "brothers" especially those who died for their country. They express their joy when they met up with another old boy and their gratitude for the letters from Aberlour and the parcels that staff and supporters of Aberlour continued to send to them over the war years.

We want to capture the simplicity of the boys' commitment, their sadness and their humour even in the worst circumstances. We believe it is important also to record the mundane events and the daily struggles of the Orphanage to provide for the large Aberlour family.

We will never know how many other letters were sent to the Orphanage but not preserved and sadly we have no copies of the letters sent back to the boys from the Orphanage or its supporters.

Many letter writers comment on the poor quality of their writing and apologise for that to Mr White in particular but excuse it because they were balancing their writing pads on their knees in water logged trenches!

We hope that this unique contribution commemorating the events of WW1 and honouring those who died from Aberlour will be widely read. We want the recorded events and compassion of staff in the Orphanage through the "terrible" war to remind us of the positive experiences of many young people in orphanage care. We also want to recognise the courage of the "old boys", their acute perceptions of the sufferings of all involved in the War and their compassion.

The letters in this book record the actual words of the old boys describing their war experiences as well as their fond memories of the "only home I knew".

If the book makes people think about the war and the sufferings of a "family" as well as the compassion of their "parents" from Aberlour then the sacrifices they made will live on.

A simple granite cross now stands outside St Margaret's Church in Aberlour bearing 62 names of the Aberlour boys who gave their lives in the great battles of WW1.

Aberlour WW1 August 1914 – March 1919

From the Magazine

August 1914

4th

We hear tonight that War has been declared against Germany. This is terrible news and will mean many dark days. May it soon be over!

The Government declared war at 23.00 hours as the Germans rejected the British ultimatum requesting that their troops leave Belgian soil.

A week or two ago a lady offered us £15 to buy a piano for the recreation of working girls in the Orphanage. She volunteered in sending the money that we might put it into General Funds if we wished considering that we might soon "need bread and butter more than pianos". We decided to leave the decision to the girls and they unanimously and cheerfully agreed to go without their piano.

Lord Kitchener called for 100,000 volunteers to join the British Army

9th

We sang the litany in Church this morning to the accompaniment of guns at sea. We learned later that it was only the testing of the new guns at Cromarty, but it was very impressive at the time.

13th

Posts are unfortunately very light these days. No doubt many people are too unsettled to think of anything but this terrible war, but we hope they will remember us soon as our bills will have to be met next month as usual.

We have been asked to lend our hospital to the Government if it should be required and have gladly promised to do so. It is an ideal spot for convalescents.

14th

We have received a letter today from an old boy just going to the front. Several other old boys are in the same battalion and we have just heard from 4 others who have enlisted for the war.

Will our friends please remember them in their intercessions?

The advance guard of the100,000 strong British Expeditionary Force reached France.

From Robert Terrell – Seaforth Highlanders - Army Base Post Office

Hope you are well. I am all right myself. We are having very hot weather here. Please address to the British Expeditionary Force

18th

A neighbour very kindly sent us two baskets of pears which will be much enjoyed.

British Expeditionary Force met the German First Army. Battle of Mons. British Army forced south, beat off German attacks but losses were high - 7800 casualties.

26th

Not a single voluntary subscription for six days.

Sea War in the North Sea, British cruisers prevented German attacks on troopships carrying Expeditionary Forces to France. Admiral David Beatty played significant role. [David Beatty was a strong supporter of the Orphanage]

31st

An old boy is with us tonight, he has enlisted and is to join his battalion tomorrow. He has given us 9s 6d for the Former Inmates' Bed.

The Office staff at Gartcosh Iron and Steel Works have sent us 10s "fines for arriving late for duty during the last two months".

THE ORPHANAGE AND THE WAR

The Warden quoted from the Guardian in the Magazine of September 1914

"The first duty of an Englishman is to do his utmost for the relief of those who are being hit by war. But it is not his last duty nor will the State be helped in the slightest by our forgetting our benevolent organisations whether clerical or lay that have long and blameless records of efficient ministrations to humanity"

We do ask that people continue to support our work.

THE NOVEMBER SALE

We certainly hope to have a November Sale and a good one. We congratulate ourselves that second-hand men's clothes, old boots and shoes and so on, cannot be wanted by soldiers and sailors, so we live in hope that they will continue to find their way here.

September 1914

The Magazine records many subscriptions being sent to the Orphanage and many increasing their donations in the light of the plight of the Orphanage.

4th

Several old boys contributed as they left for the Front. We had a visit from an old boy to-day; he looks well and has just enlisted in Lord Kitchener's Army. He kindly gave us a generous contribution to the Former Inmates' Bed.

9th

From Mrs Clark "I and some of my family are working at the little flannel vests for your orphans and hope to send you another parcel soon".

11th

No money today!

14th

Many supporters have sent money for coals and clothing. From an elderly supporter "I am trying to knit some garments for your next Sale, and I hope to send some garments which I shall never be able to wear again".

From Charles Third – Royal Engineers-Seine et Marne

This will come as a great surprise - I don't suppose you have forgotten "Tippy". We have been travelling all week and are not finished yet.

Remember me to all the boys if there are any left. We are enjoying this life.

Please drop me a note.

Yours affectionately, Charlie.

British and French launched counterattack against German forces on the Marne River.

French and British Army attacked withdrawing German Army – met stubborn resistance in what was called the Battle of the Aisne.

15th

Good though yesterday was today has been better! An anonymous donor sent 100 guineas with a note saying "I hope this will help to tide you over a bad time"

Mrs Allan, Elie, sent us two guineas, some mufflers and socks which are a school girl's first effort.

A large roll of splendid cloth for boys' clothes from Mr Roberts, Selkirk, some boys' second hand clothing, two rolls of flannel.

It is a long and valuable list of help.

16th

The mother of a farmer who employs one of our boys sends a useful parcel of clothing for which we return many thanks.

22nd

The Misses Moir have kindly doubled their subscription for this year "as it is likely to be an expensive winter with this terrible war"

Later in the month there were many donations following the Warden's appeal, money for coals, clothing, toys and puzzles.

Sea War - North Sea

1400 British naval persons lost their lives when the German submarine U9 sank three British cruisers in rapid succession.

In Mesopotamia, Basra, the region's main port, fell to the British.

Almost every day also brings a card or a letter from an old boy just enlisted or at the front.

From William Speed - 2nd Seaforth Highlanders

I received your letter and was glad to get it. If you had called me anything other than "Willie" I would have been offended.

I expect I will be in France before you get this letter, as there is a rumour that all the troops are going to sail before the week is out.

The weather is fine down here and we have a bathing parade every day. I have got my swimming certificate, thanks to the lessons I got at the Home.

[Every summer at Aberlour the children were taught to swim. Boys and girls who managed to swim round a pond in the grounds of the Orphanage received one shilling from a local benefactor]

Today we heard from one boy in Canada who has volunteered for active service.

30th

The Duke of Richmond and Gordon has kindly sent us a fine fat stag, which will make a nice variety in our commissariat.

From George Paines - RFA

I am pretty busy at the moment doing my bit. We've orders for the Front. Have been here seven weeks (RFA Boxmoor) Jolly rough living but getting quite used to it.

The Warden concluded the diary notes with this message

"To one and all the donors over the month, we tender our deepest gratitude and add Laus Deo!"

The Warden wrote further to mark the generosity of so many to Aberlour after his appeal for sustained funding. "We now have enough to carry on for a little while and we hope not to have to make a special appeal again if we receive subscriptions as in normal times."

The Warden says that he has received the names of a good many old boys who are serving their country in the navy and army.

He records that two boys had been wounded- Robert Macaulay and Frederick Morrison.

The Roll of Honour at the end of September had 35 names.

October 1914

1st

An old boy, who has just joined the Territorials, has left us today after a short visit and has given 5s to the Former Inmates' Beds.

5th

A delightful roll of flannel has come from Mrs Sharp in Dundee - a valuable gift.

7th

We are much indebted to the Duke of Richmond and Gordon for another fine stag.

Mrs St Quintin has kindly sent 12 pairs of stockings.

From Charles Third - Royal Engineers - On Active Service

I received your ever-welcome letter and have not had a chance to answer as we have been continually on the move since.

When I got your letter we had just come from the Battle of the Aisne. We lost one of our little company and four were wounded. I would like to pay you a visit if I arrive home safe.

We all hope to be home for Christmas but the chances are vague. So we will spin yarns when we see you again. I will have a game of football with the boys, as I still indulge in that sport. I can't mention much as we have a limited amount of notes.

We are resting for a while for we have been on the move all night.

Dinner is ready so I must get my knife sharp, so goodbye for the present.

Remaining with love and best wishes - Your affectionate boy, Charlie.

9th

A most welcome bag of apples has been sent by Mrs Aitken from Cupar.

11th

Some welcome pinafores from Mrs Macdonald.

13th

Mrs Christie from Elgin wrote "It is splendid to think of the boys that are now on service who have been reared in the Orphanage. You must feel proud of them."

From William Speed – 2nd Seaforths - in Chichester

I have been wounded in the side but not badly and am in the above hospital. I am glad to be back in England. Love to all.

From Albert Morrison

Many thanks for your kind letter which I received tonight. I cannot tell you how glad I am to know that the "old boys" are doing their duty well. It shows that the right spirit has been inculcated to us.

He quotes a verse from A.E Housman.

"And you will list the bugle

That blows in lands of morn,

And make the foes of England

Be sorry you were born"

When we leave for the front (we expect to be sent away any time now) I shall most certainly write and let you know. In the meantime, I trust that you will not be so badly hit financially by the war as you expect to be. With all good wishes

Photo from National Library of Scotland's WW1 Collections.

17th

Mrs McCall has sent us a very nice parcel of beautifully knitted stockings which will be grand for winter wear.

18th

Luke, the popular Aberlour Irish Terrier, in anticipation of his fifth birthday tomorrow, has received a very handsome present of £8 "to spend as he likes".

Perhaps he will like to give it to the Orphanage! He and his friends send their very grateful thanks for this generous present, which he gladly agrees to allocate as suggested!

First Battle of Ypres, heavy French and British losses. Battle of Ypres

continued into late November. Heavy rain had turned fields of Flanders into a morass of mud.

20ᵗʰ

An old girl sends 2s from Ireland and says "I am not as happy here as I was in the Orphanage".

From Ernest Partridge - Cameron Highlanders

You will be glad to know that I have joined the Cameron Highlanders. The whole of our battalion marched to Church yesterday. I am picking up the drilling all right and I like it.

I trust and hope that I will soon see you and the old Home again.

21ˢᵗ

The ladies of the Aberlour Orphanage Guild feared there would be a falling off this time owing to the war but the ladies all thought that with hard work they could better their last donations and 683 garments were sent and £12 in money.

22ⁿᵈ

We have had a most welcome gift of 40 rabbits from Mr J.C Barclay Harvey of Dinnet, which we know how to appreciate.

27ᵗʰ

We are exceedingly grateful for a roll of flannelette from Mr Hendery from Inverness. It will be of great service.

From Robert Dunbar - Cameron Highlanders

Three weeks ago I joined the 4ᵗʰ Cameron Highlanders. John Black tried to join but was rejected owing to defective eyesight.

May God bless you all.

Western Front France/Belguim

Advance of the British Expeditionary Force to Menin and Lille - British Forces held back Germans but at great cost.

28th

We were delighted to receive a barrel of very fine apples, for a treat on Hallow E'en. They will be greatly appreciated by nearly 500!

We were grieved, yet proud, to hear that another of our old boys has been wounded. He is being carefully nursed in a hospital in Chichester.

31st

An old boy, who has lately joined the Seaforth Territorials, is spending the weekend with us. He is very proud of his new uniform and so are we!

By the end of October, 47 old boys are listed as having joined the Forces.

In the same Magazine, the Warden listed the things that the Orphanage needed most from supporters.

Our wants

Several rolls of flannel to make vests and drawers

A supply of Parrish's Food for our most delicate children

Petticoats- a very useful size is 26 inches long

Caps and collars for boys

Boy's cast off clothing. Eton suits are most acceptable.

Hats for girls

November 1914

2nd

Yesterday having been Sunday, the children are having their All Saints Day holiday today, and are managing to enjoy themselves despite a wet day.

3rd

Miss Herriot has made us a present of a beautifully illustrated Bible, in parts, which will be very useful and afford much pleasure.

Sea War, North Sea

German Heavy Cruisers attacked the ports of Hartlepool and Whitby and caused 700 casualties .

4th

A friend of the Orphanage writes "How are you getting on in these terrible times? War seems too awful a thing to be allowed to happen in these so-called Christian days and the loss of grand lives is appalling to contemplate. How many old boys do you have at the Front?"

From Sgt John Anderson - Gordon Highlanders

I received your letter and was very pleased to get it and to hear that you are all in the best of health. The weather out here has taken a sudden turn for the worse and we have got some snow to keep us company in the trenches. I am sorry that I cannot come home for my Christmas but I hope you will enjoy it when it comes.

I am now a sergeant, and I hope that you will be pleased to hear it.

The Warden also reminds readers that the letter from Sgt John Anderson is from the lad who in 1912 had two of his toes cut off to enable him to enlist in the Regular Army.

Photo from National Library of Scotland's WW1 Collections.

5th

A friend of long-standing in South Africa writes, "Shame hath covered my face in reading your magazine. Here I am, out of it all. I have not even sent my subscription to the Orphanage! I have much pleasure in enclosing a cheque, and have somewhat increased my contribution".

We are proud to say that we now have 50 of our former inmates serving their king and country.

7th

We were grieved to hear that one of our old boys, Alexander Brown, was killed at the Battle of the Aisne.

12th

Mrs Dickinson has sent a useful gift of 12 yards of flannel.

Mr Dalziel, North Berwick, writes:- I am afraid you will all be feeling the effects of the war very much. However, we must not get down-hearted as that will not get us out of our difficulties, and while we must contribute what we can to the War Funds, we must not neglect pressing claims at home. I therefore enclose a cheque for £15.

13th

The Misses Chisholm have sent their annual donation of £20, half for coals and half to support a bed.

Another old boy Robert Terrell has to be added to the list of wounded but he is getting on well.

From Robert Terrell - Seaforth Highlanders

I left England with the Expeditionary Force and managed to get through engagements at Mons, the Marne and the Aisne but later came in contact with the Bavarian Guard at Hazebrouck.

We drove them before us to Armentieres. About 3 miles on they made a stand and I got wounded in my left hand. I have been through an operation and had to have my little finger and part of my hand amputated but am quite recovered and will soon be able to go out.

It is warm work fighting the Germans and they never forget to give us a warm reception at breakfast! We reply with cold steel at night time. It is by no means comfortable out there, sleeping in the cold trenches, but we just had to grin and bear it.

17th

Captain Wood has sent us a most valuable gift of 192 rabbits and 8 hares.

The war at the Western Front France

To exploit his success at the Battle of the Marne, Joffre [the French Commander in Chieforders] planned that the French and British Armies would attack the withdrawing German armies in what became known as the Battle of the Aisne.

From William Rattray - Seaforth Highlanders

I will tell you how I got wounded which I think will interest the children. It was 8.30 a.m. after some severe fighting the night before. I was told to draw breakfast, which I did with a glad heart. After getting our rations my comrade and I both being in the machine gun, sat down and had a piece of bread and cheese; suddenly we heard a whiz in the air, then a bang, it was a "Black Maria" burst over us and was followed by shrapnel which burst over our heads and struck me on the top leaving a bad hole.

20th

Captain Wood has sent another valuable gift of 54 rabbits and 9 hares.

From William Speed - 2nd Seaforths

I am coming home for 3 weeks' furlough. I am coming to the Orphanage as it is the only home I have.

We had the pleasure of welcoming one of our old boys, William Speed, on his discharge from hospital having been wounded in the side near Armentieres. He is going to spend 3 weeks with us.

23rd

An "old boy" aged 16 writes "I suppose you heard that I tried to enlist, but unfortunately I was too young. I am sure that I could have shot a German or two and at least I would have saved a bullet from a better man."

27th

Four beautiful little bantams have been sent for sale by Miss Duff.

From Ernest Lay - Machine Gun Section

I have received your last two magazines out here and am pleased to get them.

I am sorry that I cannot write a letter as writing paper is very scarce out here. I hope this P.C will find you all at the Orphanage in good spirits.

Hoping to be back to see you all soon.

28th

The first day of our Jumble Sale has been much more successful than we expected. We have 28 old boys here tonight – some in uniform and several others have been over for the day and had to go back in the evening. We have taken £212 from the Sale, a very satisfactory and encouraging result.

The Warden made special mention of Alexander Brown who was killed at the Battle of the Aisne. He was the first "old boy" to be killed in the War.

From Charles Brown - Army Service Corps

I am now writing to tell you that my brother Alex was killed in the Battle of the Aisne on September 15th. Poor Alex, he was a very nice brother. Robert and William have also enlisted and we are ready to go out at any minute if they want us. We have a good many mules in our stables and they are very stubborn, and there are a good many kickers among them. They are training them very rapidly, and they are picking up their drills very quickly.

December 1914

By December 1914 the French, British and Belgians had suffered more than one million casualties.

The magazine for December had a full seven pages of entries detailing the many gifts sent to the Orphanage in the run up to Christmas. The following entries give some impression of the kind of gifts received.

1st

A large box of toys containing one for each child in the Orphanage has been sent anonymously from Edinburgh. This handsome gift will give very great pleasure at Christmas. *There were some 450+children in the Orphanage that December.*

Captain Wood has again sent us 56 rabbits and 5 hares.

2nd

All our old boy visitors are gone. One of them is very disappointed that he could not enlist owing to be too short. But he will grow, so there is hope yet!

3rd

The children of Dundee Orphanage have again sent their pennies- "from the small family to the large one".

4th

Miss Dickinson very kindly sends a Christmas donation and says that in spite of the terrible war "I did not want the orphans to suffer: one must try and make it bright for them".

From William Baker - 3rd Seaforths December 2nd

I am sorry to tell you that I am wounded through the left leg at the thigh; it is a bit painful but I will soon be all right.

We have had some very stiff fighting and been under artillery fire most of the time.

I ran across a man who was badly wounded who said he had been in the Home. His name was, I think M'L.

I told him I had been there and he shook hands with me; he asked for Mr Jupp and I told him he was dead; he was sorry. Poor fellow he died a few hours after, just before I was wounded on the 2nd.

We had him buried as decently as we could and were hurrying away as the enemy had spotted us, and I was hit.

I am now in Boulogne waiting to be sent home. I think I am leaving tonight. I hope so.

We have had terrible weather in the trenches and felt it having come from India but we are not so bad now.

Best wishes from all the Orphanage Boys at the front

7th

The Misses Bell have sent some very pretty dolls which will give much pleasure. We have also received an acceptable present of pheasants from Lord Mount Stephen.

Western Front

Despite worsening weather and growing strength of the German defences, the British and French undertook a general offensive along the Western Front.

10th

Miss Begbie of Edinburgh has sent a very welcome present of 500 tablets of toffee which are to be distributed on Founder's Day. Miss Begbie never fails to remember Founder's Day.

11th

This is Founder's Day, the 84th Anniversary of Canon Jupp's birth. As usual the day is a school holiday and the weather treated us well on the whole. At tea-time a short statement of Canon Jupp's life and work was read to the children. Four years are a large slice out of a child's life, and only 264 out of 498 children had ever seen him. Pennies, buns and toffee contributed to the enjoyment of the day.

From Charles Third - Royal Engineers

We are having very miserable weather – we must consider ourselves lucky that we have a shelter over our heads on these occasions.

We had a visit from Lord Roberts a day before his death and another day we paraded before the King.

We had a good reception from the Germans on Nov 5th. They shelled us out of our billets but I am glad to say that no one was hurt although one of the horses was killed and a few wounded. We must be prepared for any sort of Christmas out here, for one day is just the same as another......I would like to spend Christmas with you, for I am sure that I could depend on having plenty of fun like the good old days.

Charles Third second letter dated 10th December

I have read the magazines with great interest- I remember many of the names on your roll of honour and fancy I see their faces. The Germans are proper warriors especially when there is no-one about. We are still very lucky for, since leaving the Aisne where we lost two men and had three wounded, only about six more have been wounded; many companies have suffered heavy losses doing some dangerous work.

15th

Our good friend Mr Dalziel sends us his usual handsome gift of £5 for Roast Beef for the bairns with the timely hint that we should not be extravagant in festivities this year.

We had a nice letter from an old boy from whom we had not heard for thirteen years. He is with the Army in France, in the Scots Guards.

Photo from National Library of Scotland's WW1 Collections.

From William Baker 3rd Seaforths 18th December

I was pleased and proud to get your letter and I am a proud lad to see my name in your roll of honour. As regards the fellow I helped to bury. I am not sure of his regiment or name but he knew me as he said "good shot, Baker an Orphanage boy; I am glad."

I said "Yes, who are you? He said something like M'L and asked for Mr Jupp and then died. He was wounded in the chest and leg. We had an awful time burying him as there were shell bursting all over the place and bullets whistling past. We had an awful time in the trenches, the trenches being blown in, the Germans making attacks and the rain and the cold.

I will be glad when it is all finished. The slaughter is awful on both sides. We lost an awful lot of men- a whole company in a day.

My leg is getting on nicely although I had some pain, but nothing compared to other men.

We are fighting for a good cause, and no German will invade us as long as there is a soldier to handle his rifle.

Despite several searches of Orphanage records we have been unable to identify the soldier about whom William Baker spoke.

19th

Today has brought the annual gift of garments from the St John's of Forres Work Party. The Work Party ranks amongst the most valuable of our helpers for many years their contributions have been very large and very good. The materials, patterns and selection of garments are all of the best.

From Edward Shanks - Northumberland Fusiliers

As I am going on furlough it would be a source of great pleasure to me if I could spend Christmas with you all at Aberlour. My training will be up in February when we will proceed to the Front.

While I am up so far it would be the greatest joy I could have to spend one of those old Christmases I used to enjoy so much.

21st

An old boy Emile Sieverdin, serving in the Royal Navy, has sent us a contribution for the Former Inmates' Bed.

Mrs Shearer sends us £1 from her daughter as a thank offering for a safe journey back to Russia. "She tells me they are so nice and brave those simple peasant men and so confident that they will defeat their enemies. They come in wounded and as soon as they are better are eager to be off".

22nd

The children broke up today and will be very busy for the next two days decorating their rooms.

From Sgt Anderson - Gordon Highlanders

Just a line to let you know that I am still in the land of the living. I am thinking long to see the old home again.....I have been in some very fierce fights now and had some narrow escapes.

Our lot have been up against Kaiser Bill's best troops and they tried hard to break our lines but we hurled them back with heavy losses and with very little loss to ourselves.

The weather out here is very bad and there is plenty of water in the trenches, so you can picture us for yourself; never mind we will keep the honour of the old home up and I hope it will please God to spare me to come and see you – sorry that I can't come for Christmas Dinner, but tell them in your speech that I wish them all a Happy Christmas.

24th

Another of our old boys, William Rattray, who has had the honour of being wounded in the service of his country came this evening on his discharge from hospital to spend Christmas with us. It is a great pleasure to see him.

From James Cook - RFA

You will see from the heading of my letter that I am out fighting for my King and Country, and it is a very hard job.

I often think, when I am under heavy fire, of the by-gone happy days I spent in the dear old home and of dear Mr Jupp; but if God spares me to get over it all I will be through and let you know all my hardships, for I am not allowed to tell about it by letter.

I would like to be amongst you all for my Christmas.

I have met a good few of the old boys out here and they are all asking about the dear old home.

I would very much like to taste your Christmas pudding, but I think we will be getting one or two Christmas puddings from the German guns on Christmas Day, just to remind us.

Wishing you all a very bright and happy Christmas and asking God to protect you all in such a time of trouble.

A Christmas Truce

By Christmas 1914 the soldiers on the Western Front were exhausted and shocked by the scale of the losses they had suffered.

At dawn on the 25th December, the British holding the trenches around the Belgian City of Ypres heard carols ringing from the opposing German positions and then spied Christmas trees being placed in front of the German trenches. Slowly lines of German soldiers climbed out of their trenches and advanced to the half way point of No Man's Land where they invited the British to join them. They met in the middle of the shell-blasted wasteland and exchanged gifts, talked and played games of football.

Our journal is long this month but our thanks are none the less sincere to Mrs Findlay for a barrel of apples and to Mr Findlay for a sheep

29th

We had today a most pleasant but far too short visit from another of our soldier lads, Fred Morrison, who has been wounded. We had not seen him since he left nine and a half years ago and it was a treat to set eyes on him once more. He is going back to the Front very soon.

The December magazine gave a very full description of Christmas at Aberlour and the fact that they were able to give the children a proper Christmas thanks to the generosity of many neighbours and supporters.

The Warden wrote

"We think Christmas has done us all good; it always comes in the midst of winter to brighten the dark dreary days; and this year it has come in darker and heavier days than usual and has helped to lift the clouds, at least for a while, and to remind us that there are brighter days ahead because the Prince of Peace still reigns.

We were pleased to welcome 22 old boys many from the Front or waiting to go to the Front and all wanted to have an Aberlour Christmas with memories to take back to the Front.

We missed some others who have rarely been absent at Christmas but their country needed them and they could not come; but we did not forget them.

The younger children sat down first by themselves and then 370 sat down in the large dining hall. It was a joyous scene and a happy meal and everybody did justice to it.

In the evening came the dance which was immensely enjoyed till 11 o'clock.

Altogether 564 people had Christmas Day Dinner in the Orphanage. There were the usual speeches and cheers and each child received two crackers – a gift from a little girl at Rothes. The subsequent display of caps was a gorgeous sight!

We try to keep up old customs so that old friends may be able to picture the scenes and to feel themselves at home whenever they return to take part in the festivities."

The Warden noted that the postbag from the Front had been heavy so there was only room for a selection of the letters.

Letters were also received from some of the old girls from the Orphanage.

This one was from a girl in Edinburgh

I wonder if you will remember me as it is five years since I left. My chum sends me the magazine and I do so long for its coming to see how the dear old home is progressing. I was much touched by the article in the September magazine about Aberlour and the War and thought I must send something; indeed I felt it was no more than my duty, when I was so comfortable and happy in the Home. It is not very much but it will always help a little …Is this not a dreadful war! I am glad to see that so many are enlisted. My brother might have been on the Roll of Honour too had he been in good health. He took rheumatism when he was at camp in 1912 and it hasn't left him yet. He hopes he will soon be better and is most anxious to go and enlist again.

January 1915

Several entries refer to the financial situation and the acknowledgement of the many increased donations to the Orphanage.

1st

A very good friend in Edinburgh writes "I send you my very best wishes for the year soon to open on us all. May it see an end to this terrible war!"

2nd

A priest in Birmingham sends us the yearly gift from his aged mother, whose memory and health are now much impaired and who cannot write for herself. She has long been one of our devoted friends.

The father of some of our children has sent us a piece of a German cruiser's shell which he picked up in West Hartlepool on the day of the bombardment: it weighs three quarters of a pound and is an ugly looking missile. The gruesome fragment will find a place in the school museum.

From the front George Chesterman

We have been having a pretty rough time and thank God, I came through it all right though a good many of my former comrades have answered the last roll call.

I spent a very happy Christmas out here all things considered and I thought naturally of the good times in the Old Home. A lot of us sang carols with others in the billet who sang different words but we all got to the end of the verses together. People joined in with hearty goodwill.

By the way our regiment was in a part of the line that was not very important, and on Christmas morning it was tacitly agreed between us and the Germans that we should not fire, and for once the Germans kept their word.

It is a horrible war but we feel that we are fighting a just cause, so steadily we are beginning to drive back the enemy, in spite of hordes opposed to us.

Photo from National Library of Scotland's WW1 Collections.

The weather has been awful lately and the ground is a sea of mud. We are perfectly happy and contented under the circumstances but when we come out of the trenches which we do periodically, the first thing we think of is a bath and a change of clothes as naturally we can neither wash, shave or change our clothes while we are in the trenches. I am afraid we do not look much like Guardsmen when we do come out. Well, how are all the boys? Tell Mr White that in the early days I was billeted in a chateau where there were some lovely beds of begonias. It would have delighted him I am sure.

5th

An old boy lately paid us a flying visit on recovery from a wound received in battle, the first visit since he left nine and a half years ago. He writes:

It was with mixed feelings I visited the old place, and many thoughts were passing through my head as I visited the different places and saw the familiar faces. Looking on the Old Home makes one proud to say I lived and was educated here. From experience, I know the "Aberlour boy" is much more polite and better educated than the average boy met in the streets. I was very sorry my visit was so short but look forward to having a longer holiday in the near future.

We learn this evening that Sergeant Anderson, an old boy whose name has appeared several times lately in the Magazine, is invalided home with frostbitten feet and hopes to visit us before he returns. We shall be more than pleased to welcome him.

The weather has not been at all nice the last few days and we have a good many colds but nothing serious.

From James Cook - RFA

I was highly delighted to receive the magazines from Aberlour and see that everything is going on in the old way. When I read it all though the bullets and shells were bursting over my head, which I am quite used to now, for I have been four months out here; it brings back to me the by-gone happy days I spent myself in the Orphanage.

I see there are many old boys out here fighting for their country's honour and a very hard job it is. But if the country will only dry up a bit we will give them more than they bargained for. Between the German lines and our own it is just like a sea; we should be drowned if we started to advance, but we hold them where they are till the weather settles.

I have been up against some of the best men that the German Army has at a place called Ypres, one of the most awful battles we have had, there were 8000 of our men against 80,000 Germans, the Prussian Guard, and we had a terrible lot of casualties and the rifle fire and shells were coming like hailstones; it was an awful sight and to make it worse the rain was coming down in torrents. The trenches are still full of water and we are busy pumping it out but we take it all in good part.

I am glad that you had a few of the old boys home for Christmas, for I am sure they did enjoy themselves. I am only sorry that I was not there myself.

The Germans came out of their trenches and we met them halfway; we shook hands and wished one another a Happy Christmas and exchanged one thing for another and since then they have hardly fired a shot, they told us they were sick of the war.

At Christmas we got a small present from Princess Mary and a small piece of plum pudding, which was an awful treat.

Please give our best wishes to Lady Lumsden and Mrs Findlay, Aberlour House and tell them we will remember the nice picnics we had and the enjoyable time we had together. I will now draw to a close asking God to protect you all in such a time of trouble.

8th

A sum of £2 has again been paid into our Bank by "Horse Artillery- man" to whom we tender many thanks.

We have received a most kind and gratifying letter from a lady we did not previously know, saying she had lately come across another old boy, a soldier, and from his conduct and manner had been much impressed by and interested in this Orphanage which turned out such material. She and her husband had seen a good deal of the lad and hope to continue to do so.

11th

Three delightful parcels of shirts and jerseys have come from Miss Florence Findlay: they are exceptionally good and are much appreciated.

From George Jaffray - Royal Scots

I am taking the pleasure of writing to let you know that I am out at the front with the second battalion Royal Scots and my brother is also. I am keeping quite well and healthy, hoping you are the same at Aberlour. Tell Mr White we were asking for him. I have come across a few of the old boys out here we were glad to meet one another.

I got a great shock when I heard that Mr Jupp was dead. This is all at present. Write soon.

13th

Captain Wood has sent 34 hares.

14th

Miss Cuthbertson has sent us a copy of a very interesting and simply written book on the War, which will interest the boys very much.

16th

A lady sending a contribution writes "I read about your boys and am much touched. You must feel greatly encouraged – what a shame it is that men must go to the slaughter."

19th

We have received a splendid roll of flannel from Edinburgh. Will the anonymous donor please accept our very grateful thanks?

Air War Britain

The Germans launched their first Zeppelin airship raid bombing eastern England and causing 20 casualties among civilians.

20th

An old boy sending in a contribution to the Former Inmates' Bed writes "I see that you have quite a number on your "roll of honour". I wish I were physically fit to join the colours. I was glad to read that you all had such a glorious time at Christmas."

21st

Mrs Law has kindly sent a humming bird's nest with two eggs from Mexico. We are most grateful for this most interesting addition to our Museum.

Our larder has been replenished with a gift of venison from Mr Pilkington. This will help to reduce our butcher's bill. Like all provisions, the price of beef has risen considerably since the start of the War.

23rd

We were delighted to receive from Miss Stiebal an enlarged photograph of our Founder's wife. We hope to have it framed and hung in the dining hall.

Sea War North Sea

The British moved a force of warships under Sir David Beatty from the Orkney Islands to Southern Scotland so that they could more easily intercept any German incursion into the North Sea. Battle of Dogger Bank curtailed German raids on Britain but highlighted certain weaknesses in the British Naval Procedures.

27th

We received the unwelcome news that the price of beef is to be advanced by 1d per pound.

We have received the quarterly parcel from the busy workers of Kinross Guild. The bale contained a large assortment of garments specially made for the children.

28th

Captain Wood has again sent us a valuable present of rabbits and hares.

Gas was first used in the warfare in the trenches by German Forces and later in 1915 by the British and French.

That month many letters were received from lads at the front. There is also a report about the message of congratulations sent by the Orphanage to Vice Admiral David Beatty for his significant victory.

The Warden received back a message from the Vice Admiral – he sends his love to the children at Aberlour and thanks them sincerely for their kind message.

From an old girl, MC

MC lived near Hartlepool where there had been a major attack.

We are about twenty miles from Hartlepool but there was no mistaking the noise: we all thought it was much nearer, as the whole house shook and we were glad to run outside. It is very sad to think of so many being killed and wounded so close to home. I would not like to be living in France or Germany where they are fighting steadily. This war has made such a big difference to the country and such places as the Orphanage must feel it. I am getting married in March if all goes well - my intended is Scotch and a very nice man - we are not too young, 32, at the time in Aberlour I was the smallest girl and sat on your knee when you read us stories. I look back in those days as very happy ones.

From BD in South Africa who lives on a farm at Potchefstroom

The war has cast a shadow even in this little country district. It is all very sad to think of, but it doesn't do to look on the black side all the time. I have just picked our first plums - how I wish I could just pack them up in a dainty basket and send them round the corner to Aberlour! All my fruit trees are looking very promising and my grape vine is a picture. I am making and selling butter and eggs and I hope when my vegetables are more plentiful I will sell those; but my fruit and flowers I feel are too nice to sell so I give them away as presents. I will close now and go and feed my chicks.

February 1915

2nd

The net proceeds of our operetta amount to £23 14s 4d. Of this sum we have sent £12 to the Belgian Relief Fund, and the remainder has been put to the Music Bed. This is an exceedingly gratifying result of much hard and willing work.

Despite Aberlour's financial struggles this entry shows their concern for the wider world. This was mirrored in some later letters where some of the Aberlour boys gave away their parcels to prisoners of war from German and Russian forces whom they saw starving.

3rd

We are most grateful to Captain Wood for 98 rabbits and 6 hares.

4th

In acknowledging receipt of the £12 sent to the Belgian Relief Fund the Belgian Consul in Leith writes: "I much appreciate the efforts of the young performers and their teachers. The result is an excellent one. Will you please accept, and convey, my very hearty thanks for your kind thought for our unfortunate friends and allies."

"Nancy Blair, five years old, sends these toys, and the cuffs she knitted herself to another Nancy, if there is one at Aberlour."

We have many girls five years old: they were all anxious to be the chosen one.

9th

Two old girls have sent contributions to the Former Inmates' Bed for which we are very grateful.

Captain Wood has sent us 48 more rabbits and 7 hares, a most acceptable gift.

We are very grateful to the members of St Matthew's, Meldrum Work Party for their excellent gift of warm clothing.

From Private Peter Banks - 2nd Seaforths

I am back among the old boys (2nd Seaforths) there are five of us all in the same company so it is like old times.

I was at Church a fortnight ago and when I came out, James Beattie came over to me and asked if I had ever heard the text before: it was the text written above the fireplace in the dining-hall "Remember now thy creator in the time of thy youth" so James Beattie has not forgotten the old place even though it is 10 years since he left. I had a look at the magazine from D Aberdein and saw X is a sergeant. I suppose they had to give it to someone as the most of their battalion is in Berlin! Please tell him I was asking for him and wondering how he managed to escape!

We had one man killed and one wounded yesterday. Please tell Mr White and Mr Kissack that I am asking for them and hope to see them soon as there will not be many Germans left to keep the fight up if they come our way!

10th

Mr J.P. Grant and Lady Mary Grant of Rothiemurchus have kindly sent two nice hinds, a most welcome gift.

The Kaiser ordered the prosecution of an air war against Britain, the list of key targets included docks, fuel stores and military bases but specifically excluded urban residential areas and royal palaces.

13th

We return many thanks to Mrs Raw for her valuable parcel of 87 shirts. This makes a total of 1216 shirts which have been sent to the Orphanage by this most excellent Guild. *[This was a guild of ladies who made shirts for many years for the Orphanage.]*

15th

We have received a splendid order for begonias worth £10. *[Mr White an ex-old boy and then administrator grew fantastic begonias and became renowned in the Begonia world with frequent references in the magazines to the prizes they won across the world]*

17th

We are very pleased to get a good account of an old boy: the friend who writes speaks very kindly of the influence of Aberlour on the lad.

A good friend writes "I am pleased to see that funds are not falling off, but fear the strain of rising prices for food and coal will tax your resources to the utmost, and prices may rise further if the blockade can be carried out; but I hope this is just a good deal of bluff like so many more of the German plans."

German Authorities announced that submarines will blockade Britain from the 18th. All vessels were deemed legitimate targets.

18th

The Hon Ivy Gordon Lennox has sent a large box of boys' caps and of nightingales. The caps are exactly what we need for the boys who will soon be going out.

From Frank Partridge - Royal Navy - on board the HMS Patmore Somewhere looking for Germans

I now take this opportunity of writing you my first letter since I left home. I have been in the Navy 4 years and I like it very much, although it is hard work at times, especially at the present. We had a very unpleasant visit from the German Fleet during the recent bombardment of Hartlepool. We were in the Harbour at the time and we heard very heavy gunfire but we had not long to wait and 11 inch shells were flying round our ship. Our captain made it his business to get out and put to sea but it was a terrible time. They fired at least 100 shells at us but only 3 hit us so it will show you what bad marksmen the German Gunners are. We lost four men and four injured. I only hope we shall never be caught in that position again.

The German Dreadnoughts ran away from us and we went out by ourselves.

I should very much like to come up to the Orphanage for a few days but we do not get ashore very often as we are nearly always at sea, but I will come when I get the chance.

If you know of any old boys whom I know who are in the Navy, I trust that you will put me in communication with them.

22nd

The All Saints', Bearsden, children have had another "giving service" and have sent us a splendid lot of toys as the result. Some of the gifts are a real sacrifice on the part of the donors, and we wish them to realise that they give very much pleasure to our children when they are distributed.

24th

Mrs Johnstone, Newport, has sent us a valuable gift of a roll of flannel: it is a most seasonable gift, for we are having as cold a week as we ever remember at the end of February.

J.A.H. has sent us 6 large jars of Parrish's Food - a vitamin supplement - this is a valuable gift at this time of the year. It often keeps a delicate child from falling into ill-health.

As the financial year closes we hope to have a small, though it will be very small, credit balance on the year's working. It is a matter for great rejoicing and encouragement when we consider the state of things in the country over the last 7 months. We have had our full number of 500 children in the Orphanage at the present time, and an average number in residence over the year has been 493, a much higher average than we have ever had before.

The Journal included some extracts from the Revenue Account for 1914

Food	*£2370*
Pocket money	*£29*
Salaries	*£683*
Clothing	*£388*

Costs for around 500+ children in residence!

Working on an equivalence of the pound today, each 1914 pound was probably worth £86 so the annual costs would be somewhere near £300k.

March 1915

1st

Today we begin another financial year. It is likely to be an anxious one, but we are full of hope.

3rd

Mrs Grace Booth sends a very nice second hand carpet in good condition for which we have already found a use.

4th

This is the 40th Anniversary of the opening of the Orphanage.

9th

An old boy, lately enlisted, has most kindly and thoughtfully sent us his civilian suit of clothes; it is almost new and will be very useful.

British Expeditionary Force launched a limited offensive at Neuve Chapelle, North Eastern France. Ammunition shortages limited the success and British casualties total 11,500 men. British concluded artillery fire was the key to successful trench warfare.

11th

Many thanks to "Wee Archie" Coloquhoun for another very nice present of toys.

From George Jaffray – 2nd Royal Scots, New Infirmary, Perth

Just to let you know that I am lying very ill with pneumonia in Perth Infirmary. I have had a great shake since I have been back from the front. It is proper murder out there; it is a shame to see how pretty villages are blown to pieces and the churches.

I was out there four months and came across one of the old boys, Mackenzie from Lossiemouth; he is in the same regiment as me. I will come and see you all before I go back to the Front if God spares me till then.

I am ready at any time – I am determined to have another go at the Germans before we are finished.

I had some experience of the fighting, it is real murder and nothing else; it is a shame to see the state that Belgium is in.

I am determined to have another go at them before I am finished; they should be blown off the face of the earth. At some points we were only 30 yards from the Germans and could often have a talk with them but you never know the minute they will send a volley of bullets over us so we have to keep an eye on them.

Some of the trenches we were in were up to the waist in mud and water for days at a time before we got rest. The Germans are glad to give themselves up as they are starving. Some of them speak fine English.

I will come and see you when I get better before I go back to the front again.

12th

We have had three soldier boys here tonight; one has not been well but is mending. We are very sorry to hear that another old boy, Robert Terrell, has been wounded for the second time.

13th

We have received this morning the news of the death of another of our old boys in the war, Private James Cook, 2nd Battalion of the Scots Guards, died of wounds on February 11th. He was an Irishman and was one of the elder boys of the Orphanage when the present Warden came here in 1901. He remembers presenting him with a piece of shamrock on St Patrick's Day, which pleased the lad very much. We printed a letter from James Cook in our January magazine. R.I.P.

16th

We have received the most unwelcome news that bread has gone up another penny a loaf. This is a serious matter indeed.

17th

A heavy snowstorm has come today, but it is neither welcome nor appropriate.

The final Anglo-French attempt to force a way through the Dardanelles by naval power alone failed.

18th

We are very grateful to Captain Wood for 124 rabbits and 9 hares.

From Alexander Rattray - 1st Seaforths

Just a few lines to let you know that I am in the best of health, hoping this will find you in the same. I am just thinking about the time when Lord Methuen came to the home and asked us all how many were going to be soldiers, and I think if he could only see the magazine (Roll of Honour) he would be glad.

Don't forget to tell the youngsters about this for we are trying to make a good name for the country we were brought up in and also the regiment. I hope my brother is writing to you; he and Willie Baker are wounded and I am the only one that belongs to the Orphanage who has escaped unhurt, so I hope I will be lucky enough to get through it. Write soon.

(Alexander Rattray died a few months later at Bethune but had written another letter shortly before his death)

19th

Seven little people arrived today, a big addition to our family in one day!

From Peter Banks - 2nd Seaforths

Just a few lines hoping that this finds you in the best of health as it leaves me at present. I had a letter from Alexander Rattray; he was asking for you (the Warden) and Mr White.

I had a parcel from someone marked for "old Aberlour boys". It was sent from Havant but no name or address so could not acknowledge it. If you know who it is can you please let me know so I can thank them?

Please tell Mr White that it is more like the sunny France he used to talk about out here now, but it is very cold at night.

I was just in the middle of the word "cold" when a big shower of bullets came whistling over so I will have to draw to a close as there will be something doing before long.

21st

The Bishop is spending the day in the Orphanage and is confirming 62 boys and girls in the evening.

23rd

We received a very welcome gift of a number of packets of seeds for our young gardeners from Mr Mackenzie Murray. These are always much appreciated.

The Press in the UK began a campaign criticising the shortage of artillery shells.

30th

The aunt of one of our boys who will be going out to farm service next month has sent us a kind donation of £1 with a very grateful letter which we much appreciate.

The Warden also noted that a donor had responded to the request for a piano for the senior girls but after discussion with the donor and the girls everyone agreed that the money should go to keeping the Orphanage running and not to a piano.

Following the letters in the magazine there was invariably a note from the redoubtable Mr White about the sale of begonias- a strange juxtaposition of the beauty of flowers and the horrors of the war.

April 1915

Basra - Turks took the heights and fired on the British who landed on the beach. Outnumbered two to one by 12,000 Turks, the British inflicted about 3200 casualties on the Turks

1ˢᵗ

A lady writes: "I always have such dreadful pricking of conscience when I get your magazine that I cannot really stand it any longer so I enclose £1 towards the Magazine Fund. I hope the children have escaped the epidemics of whooping cough and measles which are raging here."

We are glad to say that all our young folks are well. We have been singularly free from any illness of any kind all winter. We are devoutly thankful.

5ᵗʰ

The students at St Leonard's School, St Andrews have increased our store of clothing by contributing a valuable parcel of garments.

From Peter Banks - 2ⁿᵈ Seaforths

Just a few lines to let you know I have got a bit of a souvenir from the Germans at last. I am back in old England as you will see from the address. I have got a bit of shrapnel in my left arm, but I am lucky it was not worse.

James Beattie and David Aberdein are also wounded, but I do not know if they are home or not, as I lost them at Calais on the way down.

I had to laugh at David going up in the air. A shell burst at his feet and lifted him about 20 feet in the air and I never expected to see him again but I met him at the dressing station and he said he had only hurt his back, so I began to pull his leg and asked him if he was trying to be an aeroplane. He turned round and said "Man, Peter, I didna ken where I was for a while."

Please tell Mr White I have a French Bayonet for him which I picked up in a trench and will bring up with me to the Museum. I hope to be with you soon.

7th

The children of Inverness Ladies College have kindly sent a most acceptable parcel to our children with their best Easter wishes.

8th

A lady sending a donation to the children's Easter feast of eggs says

"Probably the hens at Aberlour, as here, have raised the prices of their eggs to war prices".

This is the case and some years ago we were able to buy Easter eggs at 5d a dozen - now they are 10d!!

From Edward Shanks, Northumberland Fusiliers 2 letters

You will be thinking I am lost, but I have been very busy and could not find the time to write. I am quite well, and in the best of spirits. Today we had our Easter Service and a very quaint one it looked in the middle of a field. The battalion was formed up in a square, and the Chaplain conducted the service from a transport wagon. Some of the soldiers formed a choir. They sang very well indeed; my thoughts flew back to you all in the peaceful little village Church. I felt sure you would remember the lads at the Front; the voices of the boys singing that prayer at the end of the service seemed to ring in my ears. The Chaplain was a good preacher.

The weather here is getting better and it is much warmer. It is quiet round this corner during the day and then at night each side begins to get the wind up, and continual sniping goes on. I hope to be with you soon, and I trust that with this glad Easter a brighter day may come, and hasten victory to us so that we can realise Burn's words, "Then man to man the world o'er, we'll brothers be for a'that."

Second letter

Just a line to let you know I received your kind magazine in which I saw some very interesting letters. We are shifted to another place now and I can assure you it's very lively around this quarter.

I noted that one of the lads said he was only 30 yards off the Germans, but some parts of our trenches are 15 yards or less. They have got a new kind of bomb which goes up in the air and the terrible din and damage it makes is awful. It is fully as bad as the Jack Johnsons. Some of the Germans got into our trench through the night. The platoon went in the morning to drive them out. We were successful. It is getting very warm here now, and it is much better than when it was cold.

The Cathedral here well I don't know how they could have destroyed it for it is a beautiful piece of work and a big one too, and right amongst all the debris stands a pillar with a statue of the Virgin Mary not touched.

One can have no earthly conception of Belgium's irreparable loss unless seen by one's self. It will be two months on the 22nd of this month since I entered the fray, and I have to be thankful for having got through so far without a scratch, and I hope I shall continue to do so. Well I shall close, hoping this finds you all well. Kindly remember me to all.

(Edward Shanks died in Cologne on May 28th 1915)

Middle East, Mesopotamia-Turkish advance on the British Base at Basra was defeated at Shaiba.

12th

Rev J.M. Fergus, Nairn has sent a cheque for £14 9s 2d, being Lenten offerings from St Columba's Church.

We also received a cheque for £25 5s from the Treasurer of St John's Church, Forres being the Lenten offerings and collections from the Sunday and day scholars.

Photo from National Library of Scotland's WW1 Collections.

We tender our sincere thanks to all.

15th

A lady sending a donation for coals says "How interesting the letters from your old boys at the Front are. It kindles one's wish to help the Orphanage they love, as much as one can."

19th

We are greatly indebted to Miss Fraser for the parcel of garments knitted by her maid, Agnes Butchart, the wool being supplied by the donor.

From George Paines - RFA

You will doubtless be surprised to hear we are in France having landed on the 18th of March, my birthday.

We are in a little village some 15 miles from the firing line and billeted in an Ecole des Filles- i.e. school for girls. We have seen a great deal of France 150 miles by train and about 60 by road.

Have been up to the firing line on special duty and found it very exciting. The Germans dropped 16 Jack Johnsons within the immediate vicinity of our billets and windows blown out. I have a piece of the shell as a souvenir

I had the pleasure of hearing the Bishop of London preach at a village less than 5 miles from the firing line on Good Friday. Four men immediately set out – our major, an officer, a trumpeter and me. The service was very impressive quite a number of the soldiers having only lately left the trenches.

I hope all your charges are well.

Kind regards to all who knew me.

Photo from National Library of Scotland's WW1 Collections.

Western Front Belgium

The Second Battle of Ypres saw the Germans reduce the British held territory around the Belgian town. First use of poison chlorine gas by the Germans on the Western Front. Many British troops retreated in the face of this poison.

27th

Mr James Coupar has afforded a treat to the children by sending a box of oranges. They are grateful to him.

Middle East Turkey

British 29th Division came ashore at Cape Helles. Very heavy attacks from the Turks and British lost their commanding lead and were driven back from Achai Bachi.

Anglo French landings at Gallipoli were a costly failure with many casualties for the British troops.

29th

A friend sends a very good suggestion which we hope many will carry out, namely, that members of the guilds and the like could help everybody if they would employ very poor women to make their contributions when they have not the time to do it themselves.

[This was the ethos of the Blind Stocking Guild where blind knitters received small payments to knit stockings with wool donated by the ladies of the Guild. The Guild then sent the stockings to Aberlour.

Blind Stocking Guild news contained the information that the Guild had knitted 1401 stockings since 1905. The Orphanage estimated that with the 500 children in the Orphanage needing 3 pairs of socks a year, the need was very great and reached 1500 per YEAR!

Many guilds would send 170+ garments to the Orphanage on a regular basis]

By this time 3 Aberlour boys had died and 12 were listed as wounded.

The work of the garden at Aberlour continued to thrive and sales of begonias were boosted after the Times of 1914 reported from the National Rose Show at Bath about "a double begonia which excited great interest. This begonia combined beauty of bloom and had a distinctive perfume".

It was one of Mr White's begonias from Aberlour!

May 1915

We deeply regret to chronicle the death of another old boy, Alexander Rattray, who has given his life for his country. He has been a constant correspondent and below we print the last letter we received from him. One of his letters was included in the March magazine.

From the late Alexander Rattray - 1st Seaforths

I hope that you received my last letter. I am still in the land of the living. I trust I shall come through this terrible war all right and be able to come and see you. I am sure you will be glad to see some of the old faces.

I had a letter from my brother who told me that William Baker was getting on splendidly.

He says that Willie had been wounded in the trenches at Givenchy in the same trench as he was in but I was lucky enough to not be hit. Thank God for it. As the motto says "There is always one left to tell the tale".

The weather has been fine for the past fortnight I hope that it will continue as it is a pleasure to be in the trenches compared with the winter.

Kindly remember me to all I know.

The next letter is from Alexander Rattray's brother, William Rattray - Seaforths

I am back in France; the troops had a good journey. It was a very exciting crossing of the channel. I am sorry to tell you that my brother Alec has died of his wounds at Bethune; I miss him very much. He is gone but not forgotten. He was always looking forward to having a holiday at the dear old Home. Robert Terrell is with me. He has been wounded twice, but is better again.

1st

May has come in dull damp and chilly and we find it difficult to obey the motto on our calendar "Welcome these pleasant days". We hope to be able to do so soon.

The Lusitania bound for England from New York was sunk by a German Submarine - anti German feeling hardened in the US.

7th

Miss M.C. McLaren has forwarded us two huge bales containing the garments made by the Edinburgh Cathedral Work Party. There are altogether 951 articles – this is truly wonderful, especially considering all the members have also been working for our soldiers. Such a gift is not only very valuable in itself, but is most encouraging to us, increasing our faith that we shall not be overlooked through the stress of the terrible war. Everything is so excellent. There is a specially large number of shirts and of these we can hardly have too many. Words are inadequate to express the gratitude we feel for this noble gift.

British attacks on either side of Neuve Chapelle. British casualties of 11,600 led to the operation grinding to a halt after one day. French reached Vimy Ridge- a vital piece of ground.

11th

We have received a splendid roll of serge from Edinburgh; the name of the donor is not given, and we take this opportunity of rendering them our best thanks.

13th

Mrs Henderson Begg writes that she has started a Mothers' Meeting at Jordanhill and that all the mothers were very pleased when she suggested they work for Aberlour. We have just received their first gift of garments with their good wishes.

From James Beattie – Seaforths - wounded since writing this letter

I know you are always glad to hear from the old boys at the Front. Many thanks for the magazine. I see that there are over 100 (boys) in the army; I think that is not bad. We are just out of the trenches for 4 days rest but I hear we are to get a fortnight this time.

We have earned a rest after doing the winter in the trenches. I thought the Highlands of Scotland were bad but I would sooner have 2 winters there than one here. It is an awful country for rain.

I often think of the old days at the Orphanage when Mr White would be cross with us for breaking a twig of a bush or tree. I am afraid he would get an awful shock if he were out here to see beautiful avenues and what had once been beautiful buildings laid waste. Such are the horrors of war. I am employed as a regimental signaller----working at the telephone at present- I am sorry we are not connected up, we could have a nice long talk but we have to be thankful we can write a letter. Remember me to all the boys.

18th

We sincerely thank "A Poor Friend" for a welcome gift of £1. This is the first voluntary contribution of money for four days and it is very refreshing.

19th

A little girl came to us last evening who was badly in need of a home and care; she had been brutally ill-treated.

[This makes it clear that abuse is not a new phenomenon]

20th

A section of the 36th Gordons, on a route march, spent today in Aberlour. In the afternoon, their fife and drum band came up and played on our terrace to our great enjoyment and in the evening a football match between the soldiers and a village team was played on our field. Our enthusiasm was unbounded and vociferous and we all wanted to enlist on the spot, but the Adjutant, Lieutenant Moodie, thought we were not quite old enough yet!

21st

We had applications today for the admission of no fewer than eight motherless children. One poor man writes "I am a widower and I have four little boys. I am sore pushed to get a living for myself and my boys, so trust you will help me as soon as possible."

From Benjamin Pritchard - 1/6th Seaforth Highlanders

Many thanks for the Aberlour Magazine which I find most interesting. We are now nearing the Germans and can hear the guns roaring and see aeroplanes hovering around. We can observe then discharging dense clouds of smoke probably to help the artillery find the range.

We are billeted in barns and lofts among the straw but for all the hardships we are quite happy. We swim in a certain canal which I am sure you have often read about during this crisis. The sanitary arrangements are not good. Sluggish canals and the water unfit to drink.

The chief occupation is farming but the people seem to be poor farmers. It is a common occurrence to see a man ploughing with cows and using dogs to pull their milk carts about.

Photo from National Library of Scotland's WW1 Collections.

Yesterday we had a route march. We left at 9 a.m. and returned at 12.30 p.m. During this march we observed many glares in the sky. This is done to watch the enemy in case they might make an attack on our trenches in the dark.

I hope you are all well.

The second Battle of Ypres concluded on May 25th. The British had 58,000 casualties since the opening of the offensive.

27th

Enclosed is my little present for your children. Please enter it as "from a friend". This is the message accompanying a most generous gift of £50.

First Lord of the Admiralty was dismissed from his post by the Prime Minister Herbert Asquith following the failure of the naval attack at the Dardanelles.

28th

A very busy, a very successful day at the Spring Fair Sale.

Several old boys who are spending May Term with us have contributed to the Former Inmates' Bed, which is very gratifying.

Western Front- British attack at Festubert ends. The British Commander said there could be no more attacks until his stock of Artillery shells was replenished. The British won a mile in depth across 3000 yards of territory but lost 16,000 men.

29th

The Jumble Sale went well and has exceeded our expectations.

June 1915

The British Government passed the Munitions of War Act which led to the mass employment of women workers. 42,000 rushed to enhance the country's war production.

3rd

Brigadier-General Philip Chetwode, Bart, D.S.O. has sent his subscription for the support of two beds. We are sorry to hear that he has been wounded and we sincerely hope that he will have a speedy recovery.

From Private Charles Third - Royal Engineers

It is a long time since I wrote. You will be wondering whether anything has happened to me. We are now in a different country, Belgium. It is a sorrowful sight to see the results of modern warfare. I will leave you to guess where I am when I tell you I have seen the ruined Cloth Hall and Cathedral. We have not yet been here a fortnight and we have had eight casualties. Things look a bit rough for us in our new quarters. Only the other night a church quite near our billet was set on fire by shells and completely ruined.

I received the magazine this morning. I am sorry to see the casualty list increasing. I have not been fortunate in meeting many of the old boys, but I live in hope of doing so.

We have had very warm weather and a thunderstorm. Do you still climb Ben Rinnes with the boys? I would very much like to climb that old hill again in your company. I never forget you nor Aberlour. Best wishes to all.

Photo from National Library of Scotland's WW1 Collections.

4th

A farmer who has one of our boys wrote "The boy arrived safely. I have to thank you for sending such a nice, quiet boy and strong. He is a very willing worker. The boys have enough to do in these times, as both our sons are at war and in the trenches".

We are grieved to hear of the death of two more of our old boys, Lance Corporal Robert Grant, 3rd Dragoon Guards and Private Andrew Healey, Seaforth Highlanders. Both were killed in the recent severe fighting in the north of France and in Belgium. R.I.P.

German Zeppelin airships launched major raid on east coast ports and London.

7th

An old boy who had not been able to enlist writes "I was sorry to read of the death of three more old boys. I knew them well".

From Driver Frank Spicer - Army Service Corps

Many thanks for the monthly magazine. You have no idea how delighted I was when I received it. I intended writing a week or two ago but as I am in the Supply Column I am out driving every day.

It is a very nice country here, but the part we are in does not differ much from the old country. We are in the quietest spot along the whole line; we often think we are in England.

The Germans seem to be very busy on Saturday nights and Sunday mornings. The guns are continuously roaring during this period.

We are billeted in a deserted iron foundry. We were just beginning to settle down comfortably, when we were shifted. We had each made little huts of iron, for there was any amount of it there. Remember me to all at the Orphanage. With deepest gratitude for all your kindness

8th

One of our old boys has sent us a French Bayonet for the Museum. It is a gruesome reminder of this terrible war.

9th

We were delighted to receive a well-filled money box containing 753 three penny pieces from Mr Greenfield who had collected the money from friends in the city.

From Driver Charles Brown, Army Service Corps

I am sorry that I have not written sooner. I am now in Egypt but would rather be in England as it is very warm here. I came out on the 25th April in "The Nile". We are encamped on the coast, and we bathe every morning and evening. Well sir, the only thing I can complain about is that we get stew for dinner every day. I am absolutely sick of it, and so is everyone else. It makes me angry when some of the men come in and say there is going to be a change of dinner today. Like a fool I

will say with excitement, "What is it?" and they will answer "Stew". I
think I will write a story about it. I wish the terrible war was over.

Photo from National Library of Scotland's WW1 Collections.

14th

Our good friend Mr George Dalziel has kindly sent us a generous cheque
for the Summer Trip. He says "The bairns, in spite of the War, must get
their outing this year. I hope it will be a success".

From Private William Speed - 2nd Seaforth Highlanders

I have been wounded for the second time but am all right again and
ready to go to the Front again. The Germans are very busy here
with their gas, submarines and zeppelins. You will have to look out
in case they attempt to blow up Scotland. They did me a bad turn
with the poisonous gas. I was unconscious for two hours and nearly
blinded. I was wounded next day at the bayonet charge, which was
very successful for us. I hope all are well.

15th

An old friend writes "I am very sorry that I cannot help the Orphanage more than I do. The times are hard, and the claims on a small income incessant. I shall probably not be here much longer, being in my 86th year.

A happy thought just struck me that I might send you Miss C Yonge's Christian Teaching in 15 volumes for the library or, if you prefer it to dispose of it."

We gladly accepted this kind offer. We hope our friend will yet enjoy many happy days.

[There is nothing to say if the books were kept or sold!]

Battle of Artois carried on to try to gain Vimy Ridge, a commanding height. French and British commanders in chief agreed that the Western Front was the key theatre of war but that they needed until the autumn to gather reinforcements.

17th

Our hearts are greatly gladdened today by the receipt of a handsome cheque from our very true friend "Inasmuch" to be divided equally between the Coal Fund, Treasurer's Income fund, Maintenance and the Summer Trip. The amount required for our one day's excursion to the seaside is nearly made up to the delight of the children.

From Sgt John Anderson - Gordon Highlanders

I received your welcome letter and was pleased to know that you had received the shell cases. I am sending two German mugs, and a French butt of a rifle. I am sorry that I missed the chance of a German helmet. I was on the road but was called back. We are having a very rough time of it but we are making it pretty hot for the enemy. They used gas the other day and then tried to make their attack, but it was no use.

I am sorry to see some of the old boys are knocked out.

I am just going to take over a sniping party. It is a very risky job but every German I see will get a bullet to make up for the old boys who have been killed. I hope you are keeping better.

21st

We have scarcely had a drop of rain this month, and the sun has been shining from a cloudless sky for nearly a fortnight.

The children are greatly enjoying bathing. Many are trying hard to swim. A lad is very proud when he can manage to swim round the pond. The late Mr Charles Baily gave each boy or girl a shilling when they could do this. We keep up this custom.

22nd

A lady in Australia writes: I enclose my subscription. It was to be a £1 but as I am sure this awful war will be affecting you, I am doubling it.

From Robert Terrell - Seaforth Highlanders

Many thanks for the magazine. I passed it round to the other boys when I had finished it. (*Robert was in the Seaforth Highlanders – the regiment in which many of the old boys had enlisted.*)

I have some lovely souvenirs here which if I could get home would look good in the Museum. There are swarms of flies out here and they are very troublesome; they pushed forward a vigorous counter attack on me lately but I managed after strenuous fighting to repulse them with heavy losses!

We find it hard to get good drinking water so we boil the water we use, and thereby keep on the safe side. The trenches are also disinfected to keep down any disease, of which there has been very little.

All the boys in the regiment are well and are doing splendidly.

30th

We were greatly delighted to receive £5 from the Rev E. Danson from the Malay States. In a letter, he says "I am sending you £5 which represents the offerings of our little Sunday School. There are about thirty children in the school; most are Eurasians or Tamils from South India. When we reach £5, I send the sum to some object chosen by the children. At least I give them the choice whether they want the money sent to Great Britain or to some object out here. If they choose a British object, I select one in Scotland.

Now it is your turn to receive it." We tender our thanks to the Chaplain and to his scholars in this far distant land.

That month the Warden noted the death of Captain Wood after being wounded in action. "He was a brave soldier and died a soldier's death." The Warden spoke of the Orphanage sincerely grieving for his widow and little son. "He was always a genial and welcome visitor and in many ways we will miss him. We sincerely grieve for his widow and little son in their heavy sorrow."

[Captain Wood was mentioned in many earlier magazines as the donor of hundreds of rabbits and hares over many years.]

July 1915

Lossiemouth

We have had a great disappointment which has however been cheerfully accepted and heroically borne by all. There are no reduced railway fares this year and the additional cost is absolutely prohibitive.

[Each year the whole of the orphanage apart from the babies went by train to Lossiemouth for a day in the summer with fun on the beach and bags of goodies to eat. They would march to the Station first thing, board the train and spend the day on the beach before returning on the train and marching back up to Aberlour]

Though we are very sorry for the children's disappointment it is perhaps not altogether to be regretted that they should have this taste of what war means.

7th

Miss Mackay has kindly sent a gift of £1 for the summer excursion. We do not know yet if the Railway company will grant us reduced fares: if not-------!

Lord Kitchener made a speech calling for greater recruitment to the country's armed forces. By the end of July, 2 million men had answered his call, many are enthusiastic volunteers.

9th

We are very grateful for yet another contribution for the treats from one who always likes to remain anonymous.

13th

Some of the boys spent the afternoon collecting sphagnum moss on the moors for medical dressings for soldiers and gathered a good quantity.

From Corporal Albert Morrison - Royal Fusiliers - British Expeditionary Force.

Many thanks for the magazine. I laughed heartily at the "stew" story from Charles Brown. Apparently we are better off than them as we have three types of stew- stew, stew and bully stew!

Last Saturday we made an important discovery in the cooking line. The cheese issued to us is of the Sandow variety, strong. By way of an experiment we fried some bully and cheese together. The result was fairly palatable.

Might this be a first version of a cheese burger??

I wish I knew the battalions and Regiments to which some of the old boys belong as there are many Scotch regiments where I am. About 10 days ago I went to a concert arranged by the RAMC and heard quite a lot of "Jocks" sing, one quartet was "Sweet and Low". This will be recognised by Mr Robinson.

I am writing this letter from the trenches, the Germans being only 80 yards away. Yesterday we shelled their trenches rather effectively. In the afternoon, they returned the compliment, but with no good result. Last night at given signals, we treated them to rapid fire to pay them out for their shelling.

I am so sorry to hear of the death of Captain Wood. He will be sadly missed.

14th

We had a nice parcel of clothes, shoes and knitting from the girls of Queen Margaret's School at Pitlochry.

16th

A handsome cheque for £36 14s 2d has been most generously sent by Mr Stewart Menzies towards the endowment of the Clan Stewart Bed. The money was the proceeds of the sale of dogs!

Women in Britain marched demanding to make a fuller contribution to the war effort.

21ˢᵗ

A most delightful and valuable parcel has come from Mrs Hamilton Ogilvy, containing serge, prints, the very things we wanted.

From Private David Douglas 2ⁿᵈ Battalion Scots Guards, British Expeditionary Force

I hope that this short note will find you all in the best of health. I am glad to say I am very well.

I have now been fighting 10 months and have not been wounded once, so I think I am one of the lucky ones.

I have been in action at Ypres, Fleaubrex, Neuve Chappelle, Festubert and now Givenchy. When I look back on these engagements I think I have done my bit.

I am sorry to see so many old boys being killed in this horrible war but we cannot expect to crush the most inhuman foe without casualties. I met George Chesterman the other day and we agreed we would be better playing cricket in the old field than out here.

We are expecting the Germans to try to break through our lines one of these days, but I would not like to be in their shoes. Kindly remember me to Mr Kissack and Mr White. I hope you are keeping better.

British pushed along the Tigris River in the direction of Baghdad and defeated the Turkish forces 100 miles from Basra.

27ᵗʰ

An old boy James Tyson writes to tell us that he has joined the RAMC and sends a kind contribution to the Former Inmates' Bed.

We have lately heard that another old boy, Alexander Baxter has fallen in the war. His Commanding Officer writes "He did his duty bravely, and, like so many others, has given his life for his country. He was working on the trench while a good deal of firing was going on, when a rifle grenade fired by the enemy landed among a group of three, two of whom including

Baxter were killed, and the other escaped without injury".

The lad was nearly 11 years in the Orphanage and left for farm service in 1908. R.I.P

28th

Mr Morrison, the father of six sons, five of whom were brought up here, has received a letter from the King congratulating him that all his six sons have joined the Army. Four of them are now at the front. We heartily congratulate the proud father on this mark of the Sovereign's recognition.

29th

"The Home Food Culture" from Penrith has made us a very acceptable present of about 60 lbs of jam for which we return our grateful thanks.

The Annual General Meeting

The Manager's report for the Annual Meeting noted that "though the present condition of the world cannot fail to cause a sense of anxiety, it is with still deeper feelings of gratitude and encouragement that we present the 40th annual report of this Orphanage.

Exactly 100 children were admitted in the year and 66 left, the average number on the roll being 491 very near their limit of 500 children resident at any one time.

The health of the children was unusually good.

Our Isolation Hospital has been occupied for several months by the VAD Red Cross Society. It has been much appreciated by the sick and wounded inmates."

The Manager also notes that many letters of a most interesting nature are constantly being received from former lads at the Front and it is very pathetic to see how many had not previously written have turned their faces and hearts with real affection towards their old home at this time of crisis in their lives.

The Warden's illness laid extra duties on the Sub-Warden and Mr White – we wish to make a warm recognition of the ungrudging manner in which they undertook the extra labour.

The conduct of the children continues quite excellent. Their cheerfully rendered obedience to authority and habitual good temper make the work of looking after them a pleasant task to those concerned. Their general disposition is no doubt due to the fact that they are well fed and housed and to the freedom of their lives, not being hampered by unnecessary and irritating restrictions.

The farm and garden continue to do well.

So far we have felt the pinch of War less than we might have expected but this state of things will not continue. The rise of prices is very serious and increasingly so. There is little room for further economising.

There are experiences ahead of us both individually and nationally such as none of us have hitherto known and we cannot tell how they will affect the Orphanage. Children must certainly be the last sufferers.

The Medical Superintendent noted that one boy who had been confined to bed for two years with hip joint disease is now at school and able to romp about on crutches!

The Education Inspector's report commented- General work for the whole school is excellent.

August 1915

3rd

An "old girl" lately married an "old boy" has kindly given us a donation for the Former Inmates' Bed.

Germans arrested Edith Cavell, the British born nurse who was implicated in aiding more than 200 prisoners of war to escape. She was court-martialled and executed. Her last words "Patriotism is not enough. I must have no hatred or bitterness to anyone".

4th

We buried today George Tipple, one of the quite early inmates of the Orphanage. He was a postman in the neighbourhood many years. He will be remembered by many reading this magazine. He was 47 years old.

We held special intercessory services at St Margaret's Church being the anniversary of the declaration of war. May the next anniversary find peace in the world once more.

From William Baker 3rd Seaforth Highlanders

I trust that you will forgive me for my long silence. I am well but my wounded knee and thigh trouble me at times.

I have sad news for you. William Rattray, after being wounded, returned to France for the third time. He was severely wounded last month and has since died of his wounds. Another boy Baxter has been killed in action. The boys from the Home have answered their country's call well and truly.

Kindly remember me to all and do not forget to send me the Magazine.

Photo from National Library of Scotland's WW1 Collections.

5th

The children have been having a feast today at home instead of the trip to Lossiemouth. For dinner they had meat pies, plum pudding, bananas and lemonade; for tea, buns, biscuits and sweeties so they did very well. Unfortunately the afternoon was very wet, which prevented a cricket match but a good romp in the house made compensation.

[It is hard to envisage the 450+children having a good romp in the home!!]

British troops launched an amphibious attack at Sulva Bay in plan to outflank the Turkish defenders. Landings unopposed but local commander failed to take advantage of the situation, allowing Turkish Forces to gain the high ground overlooking Sulva Bay.

10th

The children returned to school today and we think that it was with rather less reluctance than usual that they heard the summons of the school bell.

From Sgt John Anderson - 1st Gordon Highlanders

I am still in the land of the living. The trenches are very quiet and we can get a swim in the canal. Of course we have to take the chance of the Huns giving them one of their beloved pills.

When bathing in the canal my thoughts often turn to the pond at Aberlour. I hope many of the boys have earned their shilling this year.

I am now on bomb throwing. Bomb throwing is a very risky game. Our lot were at Hooge during the recent fighting and I may tell you we had a very hot time. Once the Gordons start no-one in this world can stop them. I am sure that you are proud that many of the old boys are in this regiment. I do not know when this war will end but we will beat the Germans come and go what likes. Please thank Mrs Findlay for sending me a parcel. It was very good of her.

13th

Miss Donald, Elgin, has sent us the most delightful gift of stockings, muffs and mufflers, which will be most useful in keeping us warm during the winter.

Commander of the Gallipoli operation asked British Secretary of War for 95,000 reinforcements. There was political dismay at lack of progress and the growing number of casualties at Gallipoli.

18th

We are very grieved to learn today of the death of yet another old boy, William Rattray. He spent last Christmas with us, after having been wounded and he and we enjoyed his visit very much. He returned to the front and last month was again severely wounded and subsequently died. Thus, the two brothers brought up here have given their lives for their country's sake. R.I.P

From Benjamin Pritchard 1/6 Seaforths

[Benjamin was a regular letter writer and was a lover of nature and describes some of the landscapes very movingly]

We are now in a most interesting part of France, the hills being like that of Scotland but minus the heather. We left our last trenches on 22nd July and marched back about 8 miles, and it poured in torrents all the way. Staying here for two nights, we again marched 5 miles where we entrained for some unknown place in our usual cattle trucks.

Photo from National Library of Scotland's WW1 Collections.

We had two wide doors open until darkness fell and thoroughly enjoyed the scenery of this beautiful country. We stopped at a certain place where the Germans have made a few reckless dashes to reach. Here all eyes were turned to England's shores. Some choruses were sung- Far frae my home I wander and A long way to Tipperary.

Leaving here we travelled a little further south to another seaport, then turned inland for 80 miles. After leaving the train at 11 p.m. we marched another 6 miles over the hills. We lay in barns resting our willing but weary bones. The Franco-German War was fought in this district, and on the hills stands a monument to a stubborn fight.

We are again in the trenches and our dug outs are in a wood of lime trees. Our worst enemy is rats and then shells. We are on one side of the hills, and the Germans on the other. It makes it difficult for either side to use rifle fire. Two of our men were slightly wounded by shrapnel.

I was pleased to hear that the Sale was a success. I hope I will be able to assist you at my old stall by and by.

I am sending you my first set of flowers. It is rather difficult to find a way to press them.

All these were gathered on the battlefield where men have fallen and where shot and shell have played havoc.

Kindest remembrances to all

20th

A most acceptable roll of flannel has been kindly sent by Mrs Johnstone, Newport, Fife.

23rd

The sub-warden has returned from spending Sunday at Melrose where he preached for the Orphanage. The collections resulted in the very gratifying sum of £13, and the congregation has most kindly undertaken to support a bed annually, which will be most valuable help.

From Frank Bain 2nd Black Watch British Expeditionary Forces

I have no doubt that by this time you will be thinking that I have forgotten all about you and the old home, but as you know, old friends are not so easily forgotten and although I have never written to you, I have thought plenty about you and the grand times I used to have at the Orphanage.

I am in France trying by God's help to do my little bit.

Our regiments and all the Highland regiments have been in the thick of it and as Sir John French, told us, had covered ourselves with glory. I feel quite proud to be a Scotchman and to belong to a Highland Regiment.

I have been in hospital having had an attack of fever. I have just been discharged from that dear "Heaven on Earth" as the soldiers call the hospital out here.

We had a great charge on May 9th (Probably the attacks at Neuve Chapelle on the Western Front, France where 11,600 men from the British Army died)

I am sorry to say that I lost all my chums in it. Our battalion went into action 900 strong, and out of that only about 100 answered the roll call that night, and the following day it was reduced to 60.

I am sure that the Germans lost three times as many; they were attacked in such close formation.

That was the same day as one of our pipers played the senior battalion into action. He continued to play until he was seriously wounded. He had not gone far when a shot went through the bag of his pipes, so he quietly took out the chanter and played with his one hand (he was wounded in the other) until he could play no longer. By that time our lads were in the German trenches.

I had a letter from John McKay. He told me quite a lot of Orphanage boys had joined the Army.

I have thought a lot about the Home since I came to France and seen the destruction. Only a year ago towns and villages were as peaceful as our English and Scottish villages now they are only a heap of bricks and spent mortar. I often wonder what we would say if the Huns treated the children in our Home as they have treated the French and Belgian children. God forbid that such a thing should happen in our land.

We must win, as we are fighting for a just and righteous cause. I trust I shall be spared to come home and see you all again. Give my love to the boys.

Photo from National Library of Scotland's WW1 Collections.

26th

Private Arthur Mylam has sent 5s as a thank offering for recovery after being gassed. He expects to be going to the front again, and we sincerely hope he will meet with no more mishaps.

From Peter Banks 2nd Seaforth Highlanders

I am once again at the front and am in the trenches. I have been lucky enough to get beside a few of the old boys. We are at a decent quiet part of the line just now, but I suppose that will not last very long. We are the first British troops to be seen in this district and of course we cause quite a sensation, as the natives have never seen soldiers in kilts. We have had a few good laughs.

Yesterday David Aberdein was boiling our tea while I was cutting the ham. He was just finished when a shell burst in front of the parapet so he left the tea and ran for his life and I had to fry the ham and get the tea myself! We are having very bad weather.

Please remember me to Mr Kissack and Mr White. I am sorry that I could not get over to see you when home, but I will see you next time, all being well.

Government ordered advance on Kut-el-Amara despite the commander, Sir Charles Townshend, believing his force of 11,000 troops to be inadequate.

27th

Many thanks to Mr Harding for a valuable gift of hares. They are specially valuable at a time when meat is so dear.

Mr Greene, Vancouver, has again sent a kind donation towards children's treats. He is on active service with the British Columbia Horse at the present time.

This magazine also had a letter from one of the chaplains to the 1/6th Seaforths. J McLeod Campbell

"May I add one word to the others you will have received of sorrow for the death of one of your boys, Alec Baxter? He and another were struck by a rifle grenade which burst behind the trench where they were digging a new trench. Killed in action seems such a misnomer for such passive deaths.

Baxter is buried with five other boys from this battalion in a little graveyard on the Rue Bacquerot between Faniquinart and Laventie. Great care was taken to make our little group of graves neat and they look well-cared for, enclosed with a brick border edged with turf and crushed brick which should withstand weeds and weather.

I gather that Baxter had no relation but if there are friends who would like to know where he lies, please pass on this note."

The Chaplain also speaks of "seeing a great deal of another of your boys. He has quite found his vocation as a doctor's orderly, he is first-rate, gentle with patients and not easily flustered, always loyal and willing".

This was Benjamin Pritchard who wrote many letters over the years.

OUR GARDEN

We beg to offer the following collections of May flowering tulips. We shall be very grateful if readers will recommend our bulbs to their gardening friends.

May flowering tulips- These magnificent tulips which flower in May, have come into prominence during the past few years. The beauty of form, size and colouring of the flowers attract attention, either when growing in borders or when cut for room decoration.

Choicest mixed in twelve distinct varieties. Per dozen 1s 6d

September 1915

This month saw a high numbers of letters from old boys from across the whole of the war areas and included letters from 3 Morrison brothers.

The Magazine also reported that William Rattray was not killed. "We received a letter from him saying he had been wounded, but was better."

1st

The month has dawned auspiciously. We have today received a cheque for £350 to endow a bed. This money will endow a bed for all time.

From Private Fred Morrison - Royal Engineers, British Expeditionary Force

I feel somewhat ashamed at not writing sooner. For an excuse I plead being busy.

Albert was up seeing me yesterday and we had a grand time together; we were close to each other and did not know it. The thought struck us that no one would have imagined a year ago that we should both be in a foreign country together as soldiers.

Looking through the magazine it made me proud and pleased at the number of "Old Boys" who have joined the services at a time when most required. Would it not be a good thing to arrange a reunion of the Old Boys after the war is finished? There would be some stories told that would make exciting reading.

I am always living in hope of running up against some of the old boys. I only wish I had one of them in my company now. As you know we always had our own petty quarrels amongst ourselves but with outsiders we were always united, and it was a case" stand fast Craigellachie"

I will write oftener now that the ice has been broken.

2nd

We deeply regret to have to chronicle the loss of another old boy in the war. Edward Shanks died on May 28th in Cologne.

Friends may remember that we gave an account in our January number of his visit to us at Christmastime.

We are also deeply grieved to learn that William Speed is posted as "missing". We hope he is only a prisoner.

From Lance Corporal Alec Morrison, brother of Fred. Cairo 6th September 1915

No doubt you will be surprised at receiving a letter from me, but not displeased I hope.

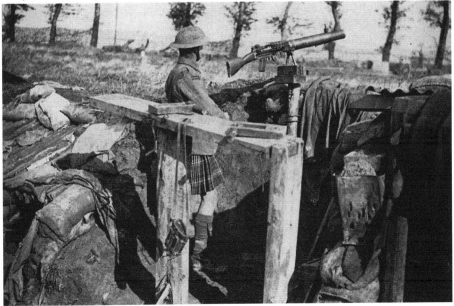

Photo from National Library of Scotland's WW1 Collections.

I have been out here some time now, and have had a rather rough time of it.

Our company was in action round Achi Baba, where I received a slight wound on the thigh. I recovered very quickly and was sent to the new landing place called Hill 971. While there I took rather a severe attack of dysentery, and now the doctors are sending me back to England, no longer fit for active service.

They may discharge me on my arrival in England or they may put me on perpetual light duty, such as clerical work.

Out here I did a lot of sniping and it was lonely work and very trying to the nerves. I was considered one of the best shots in Kitchener's Army having won the cross guns, star and the laurel leaves , a very coveted honour indeed in the Army; well you require 130 points for a marksman which entitles the soldier to the cross guns, I got 168. Naturally I was as proud as Punch at winning such an honour, so you will excuse me blowing my own trumpet.

I do not write much about the War for the simple reason that I want to forget all about it, it has been horrible.

There are some scenes I will never forget; however we will win, and then we can look forward and see nothing but peace for many years to come.

I hope everything is well with you and the home, please remember me to any that know me, in the meantime I will bid you goodbye.

7th

"A few odd shillings in hand at the end of our financial year" are a welcome offering from the children of St Mary's Dunkeld and Birnam.

8th

An old girl, Elsie Haddrell has sent us a donation. We are very pleased to hear from her and her sister Amy after a long silence.

From Albert Morrison a brother of Fred and Alec -Royal Fusiliers

Many thanks for the Magazine and I enclose 5 francs which no doubt will be acceptable when the price of food is so high. I have heard from several old boys and girls, the result no doubt of seeing our addresses in the magazine.

This war, if it has done nothing else, has strengthened the bond already existing between former inmates and the Old Home.

Miss Findlay has sent me another parcel for which I am very grateful and Miss Sharp sent me a delicious cake last month.

These gifts are very much appreciated as much for the thoughtfulness of the senders which it reveals as for the actual contents. All good wishes to everyone.

13th

Very many thanks to an anonymous donor for £30 and some most useful garments.

From Percy Atkin - Seaforth Highlanders

I look forward to the Magazine coming every month as I like to know what is going on in the Old Home. We are enjoying lovely weather and bathing in the Canal close by two or three times a day.

Please thank Miss Findlay for the parcel received yesterday; the various articles were most useful. Our battalion is in the trenches just now but two of the machine gun sections are lying in reserve. Remember me to all the boys.

16th

We are very grateful to Miss E Fowler Jones for another donation towards the Yorkshire Bed and a splendid roll of dress material.

Eastern Front Russia

The Russian losses had been great and totalled some 2 million men by the year's end. They had escaped total encirclement as Germans capture Vilna. German losses expected to be around 1 million including the Austro-Hungarian casualties.

20th

A lady in sending a parcel of beautifully knitted stockings says "I only wish I could have sent more but I am feeling that increasing years bring increasing infirmities, and I work so slowly now, but I never lose my interest in the Orphanage, and will gladly do a little for the children as long as I have any power at all".

From Douglas Rennie, RAMC, 51st Highland Division

I was sorry to see that there were some more old boys killed, but we know they died doing their duty.

What damage the Huns have done to this country. We are billeted near a town and there is not a whole building left in it. The Church which must have been very beautiful, has only part of the walls standing, and half of the tower, which is very broad and high and therefore a good mark for the Germans.

I see by Charlie Brown's letter that they are getting the same food every day in Egypt. We are a great deal more fortunate and are well off as regards food.

I was very pleased to see that you had been appointed a Canon. Please accept my congratulations. I am off to Church Parade which we have every Sunday

22nd

Miss Dixon has kindly sent a large selection of games for the children during the winter evenings. They are most acceptable.

From William Robertson 3rd Seaforth Highlanders

I am sorry to be so long in writing. I felt a little nervous my first time in the trenches but I am used to it now. I do not mean to say I stick my head above the trench to see if a German can hit me!

The other day I was in a fatigue party filling sandbags to make our trench a little stronger. I was not sorry when we finished, as the bullets were hissing round our heads but no-one was hit.

A few weeks ago I was ill and taken from the trenches to the hospital and from there to a convalescent camp. I am seventeen years old today. It is my first birthday in a foreign country. I hope the children had good weather for their summer holidays.

As part of the grand offensive on the Western Front, General Sir Douglas Haig's First Army launched an attack which marked the beginning of the Battle of Loos. The British used gas for the first time being short of artillery fire. Adverse winds blew back the gas to the troops.

Greece agreed to allow 150,000 Anglo-French troops to occupy Salonika to act as a base in the support of Serbia.

27th

We have received 40 yards of flannel from Lady Caroline Gordon Lennox. It is most acceptable as our stock was completely exhausted. We are most grateful.

From James Hay in Egypt with the British Mediterranean Forces

I received your two very welcome magazines for which many thanks. I was glad to read of all your doings. I have not seen any of the lads out here yet. We get plenty to do but I would rather be at the front. Being quite close to the sea we have a bit of sport now and then swimming. It always reminds me about the first time I swam round the pond and got the coveted shilling.

We have a church parade every Sunday. I will be talking Arabic if I am here much longer!

Kindly give my best respect to matrons and patrons.

28th

The Duke of Richmond and Gordon has sent us a nice fat stag. This will greatly help to lessen our meat bill which in spite of strictest economies has assumed alarming proportions.

British forces launched against the Turks defending Kut-el-Amara.

British troops were withdrawn for the battle for Gallipoli which had stagnated and were sent to Salonika.

From Edward McKay 1/6th Black Watch

I received your magazine. I was glad to see that there were over 150 old boys in the army. I know those who have been killed will be remembered. I have not come across anyone I know, when I do so it will be a day of joy. It is very warm. When I am bathing in the canal, I remember the day when I swam round the pond.

The last time we were in the trenches we had a heavy thunderstorm. We were up to our knees in mud. The weather is very changeable.

Please remember me to all the old folks at home.

From his brother, John McKay - Scottish Horse, Lincolnshire

Many thanks for the magazine. It is very pleasing to read all your doings. I am glad the Roll of Honour is still increasing. One of the old boys is an orderly to the Marquis of Tullibardine at the Dardanelles, and two more are sailors. Kindly add their names to the list.

My brother Edward is quite recovered from his injuries caused by a bomb exploding beneath his feet one night on sentry go. He was thrown in the air and was unconscious for a time. He was buried up to his waist in earth. Four bomb throwers had to be dug out, two of them being blown to atoms. Edward lost his cap and rifle and was badly cut. He says he is lucky not to be buried alive. By the way he met Cyril Pritchard (also known as Benjamin -so may have been when being given medical treatment) and they had a nice chat about good old times.

Best wishes to all.

29th

We are very grieved to hear of the death of another of our old boys, Robert McNeilly.

He, with four other soldiers, was getting his breakfast ready when a shell burst among them, wounding them all. Robert was seriously injured and died that same evening. R.I P.

The Warden records

"On 25th and 26th September rain fell continuously for 42 hours amounting to three and a half inches. We escaped serious flooding but serious damage was done in the district. We have just commenced to cut our corn, our potatoes are affected with disease. To add to our troubles for the first time in many years we are unable to pay our monthly accounts. We fervently hope that during next month the clouds will have many silver linings."

October 1915

The November Magazine opened with an Appeal for funds.

"Our list of soldier boys of whom we are so proud grows longer month by month and so alas does that of those whose lives have been laid down for their country. We actually have two boys, at least, who are only just seventeen now in the trenches and one who will not be seventeen till December.

Our bills grow longer almost every month. In September, the baker's bills were £70 instead of £35 this time last year. We are paying 1s 3d per lb for meat instead of 8d a year ago.

Our subscription lists are the notable exception they are down seriously. At the time of writing we have £14 to meet £350 costs at the end of the month. Who will help us?"

From Driver Frank Spicer West Riding Division Supply column BEF

Many thanks for the Magazine which I have just received. It is a Red Letter Day when it arrives. I am always anxious to hear what is going on at the old home. I look at the Roll of Honour first, and it is always with a prayer in my heart that there are no more casualties amongst the boys. Unfortunately I see the list of killed in action gradually increasing. It was only two months ago that I was speaking to Alec Baxter. Now he is no more. It is very heart rending to know that our schoolmates and chums are falling in battle all on account of the Pig Headed Kaiser.

I wish they would hand him over to the "Jocks" or Scotties. I see and hear from reports that the Jocks are always in the thick of it and if there are any important charges to make or trenches to be re-taken, they nearly always get the honour to do it. I fairly glow with pride to know I have been brought up amongst them.

I am in excellent health thanks to the Old Home, and having been brought up in the Highlands of Scotland I have a strong constitution.

I have now been out here six months, and it really seems to be weeks, we are kept so busy.

We have to keep the troops well supplied with provisions and our division is said to be the best. We convey the goods by motor lorry from the station and then horse transport take it from there to the trenches.

I hope to send a few francs soon. I am sure you need every penny you can get. I hope that God will watch over you all at Aberlour and also all my soldier chums who are serving with the various forces.

2nd

A friend from Huntly writes "I hope your great work will prosper in spite of the many difficulties that arise at this time in view of the increases in expenses and the large reduction of most incomes". There is no doubt the war is beginning to find us out, for our funds are much lower than at this time last year.

We received a valuable cheque for £100 from one who wishes to remain anonymous. We are deeply grateful to this generous donor.

4th

We are very grateful to Lady Airlie for £2 towards our very heavy coal bill, and to Mrs Aitken, Cupar, for a bag of apples.

8th

Yet another old boy, David Aberdein, has to be added to the list of those who have given their lives for their country. He seems to have been very popular with his comrades. We offer our sincere sympathy to his brother, George. We have heard of three or four others who are "missing", but we hope for the best.

See letter April 1915 about David Aberdein.

Middle East

To add to the problems faced by the troops in the trenches in Gallipoli, storms damaged several piers used for unloading supplies and evacuating casualties.

Lord Kitchener evaluated the risk of evacuating Gallipoli and stated that "abandonment would be the most disastrous event in the history of the British Empire". The Commander in Gallipoli General Sir Ian Hamilton estimated he will lose some 50% of his troops in such an enterprise.

12th

We thank Mr George Lamb and also the congregation of St. Leonard's, Lasswade for their welcome help. The Sub-Warden preached at Lasswade on 3rd October, and the result was a very gratifying £9 12s 1d.

From Private William Rattray - Royal Engineers BEF

I thank you for your interesting letter. When I read it I was very much struck when I saw the name of Private Shanks as killed in action, when I thought that ten months ago he was making a speech and spending a glorious time at the old home. Poor chap he will never be able to spend Christmas with you again. I will not be present with you this year but it occurred to me that I could take some part in it by sending a PO to help towards the grand dinner for the children.

(He sent 10s to the Orphanage that month)

13th

Here is a brilliant idea, worthy of imitation. In June, Miss Hewan in Edinburgh gave six little girls sixpence each, which they were to trade during the summer holidays. They were to buy material and make something a friend would buy, and with the proceeds buy more material and so on. The result is £4 6s 3d, which has been sent to us, and we return hearty congratulations and sincere thanks.

End of the Battle of Loos as troops fought off German counterattacks. Losses at Loos were in the region of 62,000 killed, wounded or taken prisoner.

16th

Mr Barclay Harvey has sent us a nice present of rabbits. With meat at a prohibitive price and 500 mouths to fill, this is a valuable gift for which we are most thankful.

Middle East - new commander of troops in Gallipoli, Sir Charles Monro requested winter clothing for the troops as his first priority.

19th

Many thanks to an anonymous friend for a gift of £2 and an invaluable present of stuff for girls' dresses. This donor is also very good in writing and sending parcels to some of our old boys at the front, which are immensely appreciated by them and by us.

20th

The sacks of garments from Aberlour Orphanage Guild have now arrived. The interest and energy of this Guild have not been diverted from us through the multiplicity of other claims at this time, and the gift maintains its usual standard of excellence and value. We are always excited and never disappointed on opening this huge parcel, and we tender our very warmest thanks to Miss MacDonald and all the members of the Guild.

The magazine records the items in the parcel and noted that throughout the year they had made 546 most acceptable garments.

From Private James Beattie - 2nd Seaforth Highlanders

Many thanks for the magazine which has just arrived. I am at the front again after recovering from my wound.

I read Lance Corporal Morrison's letter with much interest. He must be a good shot to obtain such high marks. I mean to beat his score, however not by points at the range, but by bullets to knock out as many Germans as it takes to make 200.

I was sniping two months last winter and am at it again. They are getting their medicine all right in the form of 303s. We have all the latest appliances for sniping.

I am sorry to see that another of the old boys has been killed. Kindly remember me to all who knew me.

25th

The uncle of one of our children has sent a bagatelle board. It will give a great deal of pleasure.

28th

One of our old boys, William Rattray, now at the front has generously sent 10s for Christmas as he does not expect to be able to be present in person. We are very grateful, and we shall not forget him though he may not be here.

30th

A most delightful and valuable gift of cloth and dress material has just come from Mr Roberts of Selkirk. We are deeply grateful for this and our eyes sparkled when we saw it for it was very badly needed.

We have had to begin fires in the day rooms today 30th October but shall not light the furnaces until we are absolutely obliged.

November 1915

Christmas will soon be here. Our young folks are daily thinking about it. To what extent we shall be able to keep the social side depends on our friends, and we are sure they will not forget us.

We are certain to have a large gathering of our younger old boys. The great majority of the elder ones have left to fight for their king and country. All will be welcome.

1st

All Saint's Day – all the children are having a holiday. It is fortunately a fine day which we had hardly expected.

John Drake, an old boy who lately paid us a pleasant visit has sent us 5s for the Former Inmates' Bed and the same for the Music Bed. We very much appreciate his generosity and should like to hear his cornet in our dining hall again.

5th

Canon Meredith sends a nice present of books, jam, toys and a money offering of 7s 6d from the Harvest Thanksgiving.

He says "The weather was very bad and only brave children could come out!"

After months of unsuccessful attacks and increasing casualties, the British began the evacuation of Gallipoli.

9th

We are grateful to our neighbour, Mr Harding, Wester Elchies, for a handsome cheque for £15 "to help you with the coal bill which will come very hard on you this winter". This is most valuable help.

11th

The last post this evening brought us a delightful cheque for £100 from the Hon Mrs Green, Newport, the first instalment towards the endowment of a bed in memory of her father. This is great encouragement.

13th

The ground is sprinkled with snow now and it is very damp and chilly, which makes the children long for Christmas festivities.

Mrs Wood has most kindly sent us 154 rabbits from Badanloch, which will be much enjoyed and will save our butcher's bills as well.

The British continued their advance to Turkish held positions around Ctesiphon. Turkish forces received large reinforcements with 18,000 men and 45 Artillery.

Britain had 10,000 men, 1000 cavalry and 30 artillery. Heavy fighting and British forces have insufficient reserves to hold position. Exhausted British reached Kut-el Amara in December but having lost 4600 men.

15th

There was a good deal of snow yesterday and there were 22 degrees of frost in the night. The boys have had some good sliding and skating today. It is the first time they have been able to get outdoors to play for eight days, last week having been very wet. *[Did the girls ever to go out sliding?]*

From Private Patrick Hamilton   British Mediterranean Force

I am sorry I did not write as promised but I am sure you will excuse me when you know the reason. I had commenced a letter when we were attacked by the Turks. We repulsed them without losing a man and then in the next few days I was too ill to write. I must have fainted and later found myself on a French Hospital Ship bound for Alexandria. I was delirious for 2 days and after a week in Alexandria left for England on the South African Ship" Elani".

Between Malta and Gibraltar we had an exciting time with a submarine. We were at tea on the 5th of November when we knocked against it, and the captain instantly signalled us to stop, and stand by to pick up the crew of a cargo steamer, the Buresk. The submarine then made for the Buresk. It gave the crew a warning to clear off by firing across the bows. They had barely got away when a shot hit it amidships and set the bunkers on fire. After knocking a dozen holes on the waterline, it made for our boat, and commanded the Captain of the Elani to get on board the submarine with the ship's papers. The enemy did not get time to go through the papers as she spotted a cloud of smoke on the horizon and knew it was a destroyer. The submarine submerged and sped away at a terrific speed.

Two destroyers escorted the Elani all night. We later learned that seven merchant ships were sunk with the loss of all hands. The next day we came across two empty boats with oars in them belonging to the other steamers, which I suppose met the same fate.

I hope all are well at the Orphanage.

18th

The first post this morning brought no money at all and we were depressed. However later in the day our spirits revived for we received several cheques amounting to £30.

At the last post a further £8 arrived at the Orphanage.

What amazes us today is that the Orphanage had a morning, noon and evening delivery of mail to a tiny village in the middle of Speyside.

19th

We are having twenty to twenty two degrees of frost nightly and there is snow on the ground. Fine healthy weather and capital for sliding, but very cold.

20th

A friend "London" has sent a delightful present of 20 pairs of excellent black stockings.

From Private Charles Walton Royal Scots

Just a line from one of your old boys at the front. I have thought of the Old Home many, many times.

You will remember my brother John. He has been awarded the D.C.M and is getting on splendidly.

We are having a serious time just now. The roads and trenches are knee deep in mud. It is the worst piece of roughing I have ever done. We have to supply munitions and foodstuffs to the troops. We know too much sometimes of what is going to happen.

I would very much enjoy one of your good old Christmas dinners out here but I will be disappointed, as I am too far up the country.

I am sure that you will excuse a lonely soldier writing to you by the light of a camp fire. I have got to do something to drive away the depression and fatigue that comes over me at times. I have no friends to write to and a letter from the only home I knew would cheer me up.

One of your soldier lads sends you the best of wishes.

22nd

We have received a magnificent gift of toys for the children at Christmas from some friends who wish to remain anonymous. They tell us that toys are very hard to get this year, which will make this gift the more welcome, and we are sincerely thankful.

A lady sent us 10 shillings which represents several weeks of teaching during the holidays. This extra money the donor always gives to good causes and she feels that our little ones must have the first claim this time.

We return thanks to the editors of The Scottish Chronicle and The Aberdeen Journal for so kindly calling public attention to our appeal.

Each day in November brings further donations, many referring to the Appeal in the papers, often small but representing the concerns of the country and beyond for the children in Aberlour.

25th

We are busy getting ready for the Sale on the 29th November.

27th

The Bishop of Glasgow is horrified that Aberlour is being made to feel the pinch and most generously sends us £5 as a personal token of goodwill and to help our need.

29th

We are very busy indeed to-day being the first day of the Sale, and there are many purchasers, besides lots of old boys and girls. The more the merrier! *[The Sale was noted later to have raised £205 2s an amazing total translated into today's prices probably close to £17,000]*

A Mrs O'Flaherty had visited the Orphanage a few months ago and noted that some of the quilts were quite "done" and sent 11 delightful quilts (2 more to come) for the beds in one of the dormitories.

The goal of the Christmas appeal is to raise funds and the volume of the postbag spoke of a continuing wish of people across Scotland and beyond to make sure that children left parentless by the War will never be allowed to want.

To one and all who have specially helped us this year we return a very hearty "Thank you".

December 1915

During the past month the weather was exceptionally wet and dismal, although not very cold, which was fortunate, as at one time we were unable to procure a supply of coke for our greedy Furnaces.

1st

The month opens well with a cheque from All Saint's Church in Bearsden where a "White Elephant" stall raised £31 for Aberlour.

It is our first experience of a "White Elephant" Sale and we hope it will not be the last! We tender our very warmest thanks to all who contributed to this signal success.

2nd

The Rector at Broughty Ferry, Rev H Waring, has forwarded additional contributions from members of his congregation bringing to a total of £110 from that town this week. A truly noble response from a congregation which already helps us most generously and has done for many years.

Words fail us to express our deep gratitude to the Rector and all the generous donors.

One contributor writes "Your magazine is extra interesting just now with its long list of honour and its letters from your old boys at the front. The letters are delightful reading as they show the happy footing you are all on, just as much "home" now that you are a huge institution as in the days when I first knew Mr Jupp and his handful of orphan boys. Aberlour has done and is doing glorious work."

3rd

The Rev H Johnston, Lochee, sends us a generous cheque for £5, having seen the appeal in the Scottish Chronicle. He tells us that he sent his last contribution 30 years ago "the laboriously collected contents of a small boy's money box". We are very grateful for both past and present gifts and are delighted that he has returned to his early love after so many years.

From George Aberdein 2nd Seaforth Highlanders

I am sorry to have taken so long in writing but I am sure you will excuse me when I tell you my pack got full of water the other day in the trenches and my writing pads were completely spoiled. The trenches are in a terrible state. We are wading up to the waist in water and I can assure you it is not very nice with a kilt on as it floats on top of the mud.

Rain is falling almost every day but so far no snow. This is my second winter in the trenches. I heartily wish this terrible war was over.

I received the magazine. I am very glad to see the big Roll of Honour of old boys who have answered the call. Peter Banks got his right arm broken with a bullet about a week ago. He will be in England soon.

Please tell everyone in the Orphanage that I wish them a very happy Christmas and New Year.

Photo from National Library of Scotland's WW1 Collections.

British and French strategists planned a major offensive on the Western Front in 1916. They also agreed to maintain their large and growing presence in Salonika.

8th

Many thanks to Miss McNaughton, Edinburgh for a kind contribution to Christmas. We have received the announcement of a splendid gift of toys which will do much to brighten our Christmas Festival. She says it has given her much pleasure to send them which we well believe, and we wish she could see the pleasure they will bring!

Evacuation of the Sulva Bay and Ari Burna bridgeheads at Gallipoli began. Successful operation with 83,000 men, 1700 artillery pieces and some 4500 transport animals leaving the area with no interference from the Turks.

British reject a call to surrender Kut-el-Amara. Turks begin to entrench.

9th

We return thanks to Mrs Wood for 38 rabbits and to J.A.H. for some more excellent garments for the children.

11th

This is Founder's Day, but being a Saturday and a wet, snowy, cold day withal, we shall reserve our celebrations of it till Monday. The founder was born 85 years ago today.

12th

The Rev Sydenham in Montreal has read the appeal and sends us 10 dollars. We also thank Private William Swanson, an old boy in the Seaforth Highlanders for five francs which he sends from hospital "somewhere in France".

Three little people arrived today, and one of them said he had never had a bath before. Is it possible, we wonder?

13th

The children had a holiday to celebrate Founder's Day. They had apples in the afternoon and in the evening we were all much delighted by a performance of the children's operetta The Magic Key in which about 70 children took part.

Mary Grant the daughter of the Grants of Glen Grant has again sent a handsome Christmas present of 1,000 crackers which will cause a lot of fun and we send her our hearty thanks.

Very many thanks to the children of the Dundee Orphan Institution for their most kind gift of 10s for "the big house".

From Private Robert Johnston -Argyll and Sutherland Highlanders

Very many thanks for your cheery letter, and for the magazine. I do hope I will be spared to see the old home again. The weather has been miserable all month and the water is over our knees in the trenches.

I am delighted to see that one of the old boys has been awarded the D.C.M. It will be a great honour for the Orphanage.

Please excuse the short note but I am writing in the trenches in a very crouched up position. I wish you all a very happy Christmas.

16th

A box of beautiful knitted garments has come all the way from Boston, Mass USA from Mrs Seeley, who takes a kindly interest in our work.

20th

Miss E.M. Grant sends a sum of £6, the result of a collection in St Margaret's Library, Edinburgh.

21st

Our neighbour has again sent us his annual subscription of £3 and a barrel of apples and a case of oranges, for which very generous gift we return thanks.

22nd

The children's school holidays began today at noon and the Christmas fever is rising. Signs of decoration are already appearing.

24th

Mrs Findlay, who generally sends the children a barrel of apples, has sent £2 this year instead to be spent on some form of "goodies" as good apples are difficult to get.

From Private William Swanson 1/6 Seaforth Highlanders

Thank you very much for the welcome magazine. It reminds me of the old days when I was at the Orphanage. We are having a hard time at present and the weather is cold and wet. We had a great fright one night while going for our rations. Some of our company were lighting matches to see what was their share. Apparently the Germans had seen the lights, and in a few minutes the shells were raining down upon us. We all scrambled for shelter. My mate and I ran into some bushes and lay there till they stopped firing. My knees were stung by nettles, and cut by barbed wire. One bit of shrapnel dropped at my feet. When we met again we had a hearty laugh but I can assure there were no more matches lit that night!

27th

Mrs Stair Douglas has forwarded a glorious Christmas gift consisting of 300 garments for the children, the work of the St John's, Forres, Work Party.

The following old boys who have been with us for Christmas have given contributions to the Former Inmates' Bed – we appreciate their generosity. The boys are:- Fred Robertson, James Adams, John Wilkie, Albert Bartell, Murdoch Swanson, Mr and Mrs Fred Childs, James Tyson and John Tyson.

The British Government agreed to introduce adult male conscription.

France and Britain discussed a 1916 attack along the River Somme.

28th

We are also grateful to Mr J.R Findlay for his Christmas gift of a sheep, always a most acceptable present.

This brings to a close, with the year 1915, the longest journal on record. Twice we endeavoured to compress it but it somehow refused to be squeezed. It is a record of the many mercies, very gratefully received. We trust that all our friends will reap in blessings in the coming year the reward of their liberality.

This Magazine also carries a description of the events of Christmas Day 1915.

Christmas, year by year varies little, but we like to bring old scenes back to the minds of those who used to join in them but are now far away. The Warden paid tribute to the many young men who could not be at the celebrations those whose Christmas was being spent in the water-logged trenches, in danger from shot and shell, or were lying wounded or in hospital. But we were glad to welcome three in uniform and others, one of whom was known for his toasts "Three cheers for the plum pudding"!

We kept up all the old customs of the season - on Christmas Eve we went to Church and sang a Festal Evensong, those who were confirmed received the Sacrament and later we sang a choral evensong. At all services, we made remembrance of our "soldier lads".

Creature pleasures were well supplied by numerous friends and the fare was the same as always. The dinner was a great success, and the cheers that greeted all the friends and benefactors mentioned in the "speeches" were truly deafening and must have been bad for the throats that uttered them. At teatime, a great deal of pleasure was caused by the Christmas crackers, of which everyone had two, the annual gift of little Mary Grant.

Then at night came a dance which was entered into in great gusto. The dancing went merrily on till half-past nine, it was rather an earlier hour than usual to close, but the next day was Sunday. We had several more dances during the week.

Christmas trees for the young ones have become an institution and are very much enjoyed. There were three this year, and the very considerable labour but willing labour bestowed upon decorating them was well repaid; they were certainly very beautiful.

We sincerely thank all who by gifts or labour contributed to a very bright Festival and we wish them all a Bright New Year.

January 1916

The Warden opens the magazine with a note about a visit from an old boy who left us rather more than four years ago. He was at the Sulva Bay landing, and his account of his experiences there is thrilling indeed. He was one of those who had to swim ashore from the lighters with shells dropping all around. At one time the men were three days without food and were glad to chew some wax candles which they happened to find to quench their thirst. He never expected to return home again, and cannot understand how they escaped with their lives. He describes the Turks as extremely good shots, and says it was a marvel how they managed to pick off periscopes above the trenches. On one occasion, a Turk, hidden behind a bush, made a thrust at him with a bayonet. He caught sight of it and instinctively dropped the butt of his rifle on it: the point of the bayonet just pricked his leg and made a slight wound, which the flies bothered for some days; but he shot the Turk!

We little thought when this lad left the Orphanage, what he would go through within those four years; and he talks about it as simply as if it were a football match!

1st

New Year's Eve was a great time; we had a dance according to old custom, and the pleasure of the evening was much enhanced by the visit of some of the wounded soldiers from our Isolation Hospital, one of whom played the pipes for the Reel.

Exactly at midnight the dancing ceased and we sang Auld Lang Syne and then dispersed to bed among much cheering.

We were not too tired to be at church at quarter to eight in the morning to dedicate the New Year to God and to seek his blessing on us.

The British ended their highly successful submarine campaign against Turkish shipping.

Some 50% of Turkish merchant ships have been sunk and the rest were short of fuel.

3rd

"Inasmuch" sends us another handsome gift of £40; half to the general funds and half for coals and 1s 9d anonymously from Edinburgh

The British launched their first attempt to reach Kut-el-Amara. Turkish troops outnumbered British troops. As the troops neared Kut –el Amara they were put onto half rations but an unknown store of barley relieved the position somewhat.

5th

We sincerely thank Mrs Cotton from Leyland for a welcome gift of coal in lieu of stockings.

Driver Walton has been very much touched by the many gifts he has received from friends, known and unknown, since his first letter was published in our magazines.

We know that one or two had taken pity on his loneliness and sent him presents and letters, but there have been more than we had any idea of.

He writes most gratefully to those whose addresses are known.

I cannot find words to express my appreciation and thanks for their generous gifts and wishes. My comrades and I have done justice to their good things. I have never thought I had so many friends as the last two weeks have brought me. My name has been in the mail every day for the past weeks

We add our sincere thanks for the kindness which has been shown him.

6th

Mrs J.L. Wood has sent us another valuable present of 84 rabbits and 7 hares for our larder.

7th

The Duke of Richmond and Gordon has sent us a welcome gift of 48 rabbits.

From Private Arthur Mylam 2nd Seaforths

Many thanks for the magazine which came yesterday. I was looking forward to its coming more eagerly than ever, for it is so nice to hear from the "old home", more especially out here.

The trenches are as bad as ever, mud knee deep, in fact, I believe deeper, only our kilts spread out and keep us from going further. We are a rare picture going along a trench, legs out of sight and kilt spreading or floating, forming a carpet on top.

We only do four days in and four days out; but the four we are out are doing hard labour it is, cleaning ourselves and just going back for the same thing. The weather is very wet and it is frosty at night.

I have seen Terrell and Aberdein since coming out as the 1/6th Seaforths are lying close by. I hope you are all well after your

Christmas treat and will remain so until I can call on you again, which will, I trust, not be long.

I was just thinking I could hear Mr White saying "Oh Mylam, what writing, do write better" just as he used to do in Botany. But I am sure you and he will excuse me this time as my desk is my knee and I am far from being in a comfortable position. Remember me to all.

The evacuation of Gallipoli was completed but the campaign had cost British, French and Commonwealth troops some 250,000 men and the Turks some 250,000.

10th

Other most welcome gifts are £3 from Mrs Stretell, £5 and a parcel of garments from Miss Dickinson; £1 from the children of Portree, 10s from Nurse Tait and 5s from Misses Espinasse.

We have a valuable present of tweed ends from Colonel Porteous of Portree. These pieces are of great value to us and we are at work on them already.

11th

Another valuable gift has come today, a nice hind from Mr Grant of Rothiemurcus, for which we return many thanks.

13th

The children of Dalry Mission, Edinburgh have kindly sent us 5s 9d.

Miss McIntyre sends 12 most excellent scarves which have been made by the girls of the Sunday School of All Saints Church, St Andrews.

15th

Mrs St Quinton has sent us a valuable gift of three rolls of serge, which will make excellent dresses for some of our girls.

From Corporal Albert Morrison – one of 5 brothers in the war

At present I am at the Divisional School of Instruction a few miles behind the firing line. Some people have us believe that there is no organisation in the British Army – they ought to be made to wear gas helmets for the duration of the war!

My company was detailed as Army Corps HQ Detachment. It was great. We saw Sir John French and Sir Douglas Haig, the former of whom inspected our guard and congratulated us on our smartness.

The Corps Commander wrote a very congratulatory letter to our Colonel who fairly beamed on us when we returned to the battalion.

I am so glad that your appeal met with such a ready response, and trust another will not be necessary during the war.

Eight Petty Officers from some of our Dreadnoughts spent a night in the trenches with us, so that they could go back and tell their mates what it was like. I heard one remark to another, "Give me the high seas, Bill, this is hell"

All the same this navy is going to win the war for us – without it the army would not have a ghost of a chance.

With all best wishes for the New Year

18th

Private Leonard West who is on short furlough from the front, has kindly sent us 5s for the Former Inmates' Bed, we hope he will pay us a visit.

20th

Many thanks to Mrs J.P. Wright for her valuable gift of £10 and for her kindness to one of our old boys, a soldier.

From Private Frederick Morrison -Royal Engineers

Many thanks for the magazine and the cocoa, both to hand this morning. The mag was given to a man named Harrison a few days ago in mistake. I usually read the mag from cover to cover.

The cocoa is much appreciated and if you could only see us making it you would be highly amused; the fire is made in a pail with holes punched all round to make sufficient draught for the fire to burn. There are usually 5 or 6 of us sitting round the fire, mess tins full of water on top all bent on making something to drink before turning in.

The YMCA hut is nearby and at nights there are sing-songs. Sports have been arranged and so far we have played two football matches, the honours resting with us. A Christmas dinner has been arranged by the officers to take place in town. This is a very nice place- all around are the Alps with snow capped peaks. When the sun sets at night it is a lovely sight; yet with all the beautiful scenery, sports and Christmas dinner, I would far sooner be at the Old Home for Christmas Day and dance the polka as of old at night.

My thoughts will be with you this Christmas and I hope that the coming year will be one of peace, prosperity and happiness- that is the sincerest wish of another of your family.

21st

Many thanks to Miss Barnett, Holdenbury, for a grand parcel of garments for the children.

Also to a "working lass", Edinburgh, for a welcome contribution of 1s.

25th

Bombardier George Paines has sent a generous gift of 15 francs.

From Bombardier George Paines - 18th London Battery

I write to thank you for the tin of cocoa you sent me at Christmas.

It arrived at a very opportune moment; we were in action (we still are) in what one would call a "hot shop" at the time. It necessitated us remaining at our guns until the very early hours, morning after morning. The rain and wind as a rule waste but little time in entering our gun emplacements, with the result that one is, more often than not, pretty wet from head to foot. I must state though, in case of complications with many of the old boys in our "glorious infantry" that we are having a holiday in comparison..

Cocoa, hot, in these circumstances is absolutely "tres bon".

We spent a fairly quiet Christmas but were up 4 consecutive nights during Christmas week till 3 or 4 a.m. We let the Huns have shrapnel, high explosive shells until past 7 a.m. This was in order to upset a contemplated attack: thus, we greeted the New Year.

Our thoughts wandered back to the Homeland and we could easily visualise what our nearest and dearest were doing far from the noise and death-dealing missiles.

I thought of you all in the "Old Home" on Christmas Day and fancied I could hear those after-dinner speeches and round after round of cheers. I could see the well-laden tables and rows of smiling faces. Please give my best wishes to everyone at the old home and tell them to cast out of their minds the vision of Huns digging trenches on the lawn or marching up the drives.

Photo from National Library of Scotland's WW1 Collections.

The war is sailing along quite all right, and provided we are given plenty of munitions and men, we shall manage, at least to keep the Huns well occupied where they are at present. I shall be glad to see this horrible war over but pro tem it's our business to see it through and with the help of God we shall.

I am sending you a few francs for the Former Inmates' Bed. I hope you will soon have all you require. I am immensely pleased and proud to see that one of our boys has won the D.C.M. Please tell Mr White I have some souvenirs for his Museum.

26th

We have received a most excellent parcel of children's garments from the ladies of St Matthew's, Meldrum Work Party.

27th

A very acceptable gift of 64 rabbits has come from Badanloch from Mrs J.L. Wood, for which we return many thanks.

From Private Matthew Jack, Trench Mortar Battery Royal Garrison Artillery

I have seen James Duncan; he is in the 7th Royal Scots Fusiliers. I was with him last night and I gave him the last two magazines sent to me. Some of our Battery has been away on pass but I do not expect one as I have been away on account of my father's death.

It was a big blow for me when I got word of it. He was the only one at home beside Robert and here I am and I do not know when I may go but I don't look at it that way.

I always say "Keep your heart up and your head down". I will send you a few francs when I can.

I will close my letter with my best love to all at the Home.

28th

We thank most sincerely Miss E.K. Thorpe for a contribution of stocking dolls which will greatly amuse our little ones.

German airships launched their first attack on central and north west England, key industrial areas.

February 1916

Note from the Warden

Bombardier George Paines who writes such capital letters, has been brought back from the Front to do engineer work for the Government at home. He admits there are certain advantages in the change, but is in two minds about it. He says

"Really, I have a few misgivings about returning: I should like to be in at the finish, which, I am positive, won't be long now. Still I shall continue doing my little bit by assisting to make the guns and ammunition necessary for their complete, I was going to say, annihilation."

Several of the letters from the Old Boys are clearly written in late 1915 but had not been received till well into 1916 - hence the many references to Christmas!

1st

The first contribution of the month is one of £3 15s from the Sunday Scholars of St Andrew's Cathedral, Aberdeen to whom we are most thankful for their kind gift.

4th

We are grateful to Miss Gertrude Curtis for her kind gift of a guinea for coals.

From Private Thomas Parsons - Mediterranean Forces

I am sorry not to have written before but will not try to excuse myself as I have really no excuse to give except laziness.

I joined the Scottish Horse on the day war was declared and was immediately taken from the Regiment and posted to the Brigade Staff on which I have been since.

We have been out here a month now and I can tell you it is pretty hot! Being on the staff I do not go into the firing trenches but I wish I did as it is safer there than behind for though you do not get so many rifle bullets you make up for them with shells, yet taken all round we are quite cheerful and though living underground we are quite comfortable. Willie Beard is also in the Scottish Horse but did not see him until we met on the boat coming here. There may be others as well whom I have not met. Beard and I were just trying to think how many old boys had joined up and we came to the conclusion there cannot be short of 300. We will not all be able to meet again but what a day it would be if all the old boys who have been through it could arrange to meet at the old home where in peaceful times there was always a welcome for us and someone always eager to listen to how we had been. Please tell Mr White and the rest of the staff I was thinking of them and asking for them.

Please tell the boys that in this trying time that they give you as little trouble as possible and though they are too young to fight, they can rest assured that we will do it for them.

Western Front

The British deployed their first single-seater squadron.

8th

Winter is returning after a spell of mild weather, and we have deep snow today.

German assault on the French at Verdun was postponed because of the snow and rain.

12th

Many thanks to Mrs Bald from Eaton Square for her welcome contribution of £2, half for coals and half for the general fund.

Private John Black has considerably helped the Former Inmates' Bed by a handsome gift of £2. He tells us he has taken some time to save it up out of his pay, which we can well believe and we much appreciate his generosity.

He expects to be leaving for the front immediately.

From Private John Black - Seaforth Highlanders

I am writing to let you know this will be my last letter for some time as I am now on my way to Mesopotamia, but I hope to send you a note when we arrive there.

I can assure you we are a jolly lot as we go sailing along, and if you could see us with our yellow uniform helmets it would cure anyone with sore eyes.. We sing songs of every description; there is one I am particularly interested in, and that is "Are we downhearted," then comes the soldier's boy cry "No" and a very big one it is!!

We are having glorious weather and I am sure we will not be bothered by cold hands and feet. I fancy I can see the sweat falling from us like snowballs when we chase the Turks out of Baghdad.

Kenneth MacKenzie has enlisted. Aberlour Orphanage boys forever! May they all be spared to come through this awful war and see the Old Home again?

If I get wounded I am afraid I shall be boxed in Mesopotamia for the duration of the war. I will not like that but will grin and bear it.

I enclose £2 which I have saved since I joined the Army and my belongings are at Nairn. I leave them all to you if I do not return. Farewell.

Sadly John Black did not survive the War and have his wish granted to see his old home again.

13th

This is the fifth anniversary of our Founder's death, and it was specially commemorated in our Church Services.

Britain and France confirmed that there could be no peace with Germany without the restoration and guarantee of Belgian neutrality.

15th

Many thanks to Mrs Heron Wilson for a very excellent parcel of children's clothing.

The members of a local Work Party have been good enough to send parcels to twelve of our old boys at the front. We very much appreciate this kind act as will they.

16th

Mr Baxter of Teasses sends a cheque for £10 and says "All charities must suffer during the war and perhaps after but I hope Aberlour will weather the storm."

18th

We have this morning received a most handsome gift of £100 for the War Loan bed from J.A.H. to whom we have previously been indebted for several generous benefactions. We have just received a grand parcel of 77 excellent shirts from Mrs Raw and the members of her Shirt Guild. The Guild is one of the most valuable of our aiding Societies and we are most grateful to all the members for their very great assistance.

19th

Four little sisters arrived today, the eldest only 4 years old! No twins among them! Some of them look very delicate and will need great care. They arrived in a snowstorm with about six inches of snow on the ground!

From Private R Johnston, Argyll and Sutherland Highlanders.

I thank you very much for the nice present I received today. It is very good of you to think of me. Cocoa is much enjoyed out here.

I am pleased to tell you that we are out of the trenches for a month, and we are lying in comfortable billets, well away from the firing line. We had an exciting time coming out of the trenches and I thought I was finished, as I was blown up in the air by the concussion of a shell, but I am all right now with the exception of a few bruises. I am thankful that I shall be safe for a time at least. I am glad that you did well at the Sale. I wish I had been there, for I did enjoy myself every half year when I came from Nethy Bridge.

I send my kindest remembrances to all at the Old Home.

21st

We return sincere thanks to the Rev Sydenham Lindsay from Montreal, Canada for very kindly sending us the sum of 10 dollars. It is most acceptable to us.

We are also grateful to Miss Hughes who sends us her 10s subscription from Saggidha, Punjaub.

Russia decided to launch an offensive on the Eastern Front to relieve some of the pressure on the French who were fighting for their lives in Verdun.

One of the key French positions at Verdun fell to German troops. General Petain was appointed and improved supplies to the troops. Units suffering heavy casualties were withdrawn to rest and recuperate.

A sudden thaw at the end of February turned the shell blasted battlefield at Verdun into a morass.

29th

This is the last day of our financial year. We are deeply grateful to all the friends who have helped us so much in these trying and anxious times. We very much hope that many of those who came to our help in the autumn for the first time will see their way to giving us annual help and that will do more than anything else to stave off another crisis.

The magazine also gave details of the continuing work of the Blind Stocking Guild. The Guild started in 1905 and since that time 1623 pairs of stockings had been knitted by the blind and sent to the Orphanage. Each member of the Guild subscribes 1s or more a year. With the money collected, wool is purchased and blind persons paid for the knitting into stockings. Each pair costs 2s with 1s for the wool and 1s for the blind knitter.

The Guild is invaluable to us as we require over 1500 pairs of stockings each year and the employment it gives to the blind is so much appreciated by them that Miss Varty Smith would be glad if she had double the number of subscribers.

The March magazine gave the financial details for the year ending March 1916. The expenditure was split into Maintenance and Administration

From Maintenance:-

Some interesting sums

Provisions and household stores	*£2681*
Farm Account cost of stock etc	*£492*
Garden Account	*£112*
Clothing and linen	*£330*
Fuel	*£470*
Lighting	*£84*
Summer outings	*£70*
Pocket Money	*£35*
Rents and rates	*£277*
Salaries and wages	*£874*
Repairs	*£272*

From Administration	
Warden's stipend	*£200*
Treasurer's stipend	*£200*
Sub warden's stipend	*£50*
Printing travel etc	*£127*

We need to bear in mind that, for example, the pocket money of £35 had to be shared among probably 300 children of an age to receive pocket money-£3 per month - so the children would receive around 2 pence a week. Some calculations on the equivalent value of £1 in 1914 with today's prices say that £1 would be £86 in current monetary value.

So the total annual costs of running the Orphanage for 450+ children would equate to £228,674.

March 1916

2nd

Miss Stafford has kindly sent £10 10s for the support of a child. The little girl Miss Stafford has been supporting leaves shortly, we hope that another will be "adopted" in her place.

The Government announced that all single men aged 18 – 41 were liable for compulsory military service.

From Private George Jeffrey - 1st Royal Scots Salonika Forces

I am sorry not to have written to you before this but we have been very busy. I had a Church Parade today. Our Brigade General and staff were present. We had a very interesting service but it did not last long enough as the Chaplain had other services to attend to.

I thank you for the magazines – they are doubly welcome here as we receive very little reading material. We are on the hills of Greece and we have made little dug outs. I have a nice fire in mine. The chimney is made out of a biscuit tin. It would be a bad lookout for us if the Germans came over with an aeroplane and took our chimneys as the muzzle of a gun and dropped an iron foundry on top of us; that is about all they are good for as they are afraid to come out and fight fair and square.

I saw a grand sight the other day. Quite an array of aeroplanes passed over our heads. I think they were on their way to make a raid on the Bulgarians. They gave a fine performance in the air.

I hope to send you later a little help towards paying your bills. They must be so heavy when food is so dear.

Will you please convey my sincere thanks to the kind lady who sends me parcels? They are most welcome as we are in quarters where it is difficult to obtain anything. Please give my love to all in the old Home.

6th

Mrs Seely, Boston, Mass. U.S.A. has again sent us a nice box of children's garments and we are very glad it escaped all submarines.

7th

Thanks to Mrs Wood for 70 rabbits and 2 hares.

We have been deeply grieved today to learn of the early death of Robert Johnstone another of our "heroes" who was shot through the head by a sniper when on sentry duty on 1st February. Only last month he wrote that he was out of the trenches for a month and safe for a time.

Alas how short a time! He was only 17! It is less than three years since he was a boy here. He was a bright, merry lad and he will long be remembered by his contemporaries for his singing and acting in our first two operettas.

10th

We have had deep snow for more than a month and it seems to have been as bad almost everywhere.

From Colin Allan - Canada

Many thanks for your letter. We have had a very severe winter. Since New Year the thermometer hovered between 30 and 40 below zero.

I see that quite a lot of the old boys are in the army and some have shown their worth. The anti-German feeling here is very strong and riots have occurred. All aliens have been expelled from the big business houses.

I shall be very pleased to receive the magazine. The mention of it brings back the old days when we used to lick gum by the mouthful. (A reference to the boys' involvement with the distribution of the

Aberlour magazines) I often wonder why the authorities do not put some kind of breakfast food on the wrappers. It would serve a double purpose, that of feeding and sticking at the same time.

Business is flourishing since the fire in Ottawa. We have a contract to install a fire alarm system in the Provincial Government Buildings here.

We send our kind remembrances to all who knew us.

11th

Mrs Mackenzie Murray has again sent a present of some packets of flower seeds for the children's gardens. We hope that the weather will soon clear so that they can begin to get the gardens ready.

We are very grateful for a valuable roll of flannel sent anonymously from Edinburgh.

15th

We are very grateful to Mrs J.B. Clark, Little Aston Hall for some beautiful scarves and to Miss Dickinson of Edinburgh for a useful parcel of petticoats.

The Russians launched a major offensive designed to aid the French, who were struggling to halt the major German offensive on Verdun. Russians suffered heavy losses and resorted to attacking under cover of darkness.

Major Russian advances bogged down in water-logged terrain and the Battle of Verdun raged till Mid-April.

21st

We are very grateful indeed to Mrs Henry Tod, Edinburgh for 10 bottles of Parrish's Chemical Food. This is always a most acceptable gift for we find it very excellent for some of our frail children.

From Private James Beattie - 2nd Seaforth Highlanders

Many thanks for the magazine which I received quite safely. It is ever on my mind to write oftener but I am kept busy and the days slip by so quickly.

While I am in the trenches I am kept steady at it from sunrise to sunset, waiting for my chance to bag a Hun. I have been a sniper for months. When we are in billets I am generally out practising, to be able to register a hit at any range.

The trenches we are in are only 30 yards apart and on the first day the Germans had it all their own way. However, when darkness set in, I made a nice sniping loop-hole and scored a Hun the first shot and then I took three periscopes in succession. There would be plenty of grousing when it got smashed as they are expensive.

I am keeping in the best of health and enjoying myself. I hope to be going on furlough soon. I am greatly interested in reading the old boys' letters. I wish them all the best of luck as all the other writers express the desire to have a reunion at the Old Home after the war is over. I trust their wishes will be gratified.

22nd

We are most grateful to Mrs Tod for her annual subscription and a kind offer to write to one of our lads now in Mesopotamia.

In the Atlantic, the British ship Farnborough disguised as a merchant ship sank a German U 68.

25th

We had a very pleasant but short visit today from an old boy whom we have not seen for ten years. Like so many others he was in the King's uniform. He has been in Australia and America and is now farming on his own behalf.

27th

We have been asked to take two black babies! We have had a Cingalese boy for the last 9 years and he is thriving well.

April 1916

1st

The month has dawned mild and genial and free from snow; the boys are able to make a beginning at their gardens and digging is in full swing today.

Miss C.S. Anderson has kindly sent £1 for coals and a parcel of remnants, both very acceptable.

Sea War Adriatic

Largest evacuation to date involved removal of Serbian forces from Albania some 260,000 troops. 19 French, British and Italian warships sunk in air and submarine attacks.

6th

Four of our young people have left us today for friends in Canada. We trust they will get safely across the Atlantic.

From Private William Robertson - 1st Seaforth Highlanders Indian Expeditionary Force

I am sorry for being so long in writing but I am sure you will excuse me when you know that we have left France and are now in the East fighting the Turks on the banks of the Tigris.

I can assure you it is not altogether a cake walk, as we have more than one enemy to face, the Turks, heat and disease.

So far I have escaped but one never knows when one's turn may come. I am afraid that Frank Bain of the Black Watch is either killed or wounded. It is nearly a month since we parted. It was a very sad goodbye, but we had to put up with it.

We spent a very quiet Christmas and New Year but we all made the best of it. I was wondering how many of the old boys were present that had been at Christmas dinner in 1914.

We see by the papers that the war may not last much longer, but no one can foretell what is to happen. We all hope for a speedy ending and that the world may be at peace for many years to come.

I trust all are well at the dear "Old Home".

P.S. I have made further enquiries about Frank Bain. I find he was wounded on 7th January.

Middle East - British suffered heavy losses as they tried to reach Kut, slow progress and further fighting near Kut led to British troops losing their previous advantages.

8th

Very many thanks to Miss Stevenson for 10s from her box at the George and Abbotsford Hotel in Melrose.

11th

We are most grateful to Mrs J.L. Wood for a useful gift of 54 rabbits and 11 hares. Our best thanks to Miss Batters for a guinea towards the "Easter Pudding".

Unsuccessful Russian offensive around Lake Naroch ended. Russians counted 122,000 casualties, Germans lost 20,000 men.

15th

Mrs Fergus has sent us an acceptable parcel of garments from St Columba's, Nairn; it contains some stockings, which are particularly valuable just now, as we have very few indeed in our store.

British Aircraft dropped food supplies to the besieged British Garrison at Kut-el-Amara.

17th

An old boy, Murdoch Swanson, is here for the night and has kindly given us 5s for the Former Inmates' Bed.

20th

All gifts are welcome and for all we are truly grateful, but sometimes there comes one which, for some reason, is particularly good. Such is the one received today from Mrs Sanctuary, Somerset. Just before it arrived we had realised that we had not socks and big shirts to fit out more than a third of the boys who will be leaving us for work in the next two or three weeks. There seemed nothing for it but to buy the things at great expense; ten minutes later all the very garments that we sorely needed lay before us, the contents of six splendid parcels from Mrs Sanctuary! Our hearts fairly danced for joy; it was almost as if Mrs Sanctuary and her friends had been told the exact number of boys whom we had to rig out!

21st Good Friday

Miss Hadley sent us some Calvary cloverseed pods, the development of which we will watch with much interest.

From Private William Thain – Norwich

Thank you so much for sending me the magazine It gives me great pleasure to read the news concerning the Old Home.

It was very sad about the death of Robert Johnston. It seems but yesterday that we played in the fields together. It is hard to think that we will never see him again on earth.

Norwich is a bit noisy at night and it is dark as a coal cellar in the East Block. It is darkened on account of the Zeppelins, which come this way pretty regularly. I see they have been in Scotland, but it is to be hoped they will never come as far north as you, for it would be terrible to think what would happen to all the young lives under your roof.

Easter is here once more and I am sure it will be enjoyed by all the inmates of the Orphanage. I often wish I was younger and back again but "Time and Tide wait for no man" Kindly give my love to all who know me.

25th

We are very grateful to Miss Sharp of Broughty Ferry for £1 towards the summer trip. We wonder, will there be a "Lossie" this year?

Four German Battle cruisers bombed Great Yarmouth and area. German ships made hasty retreat with the surprise arrival of British Naval Forces.

27th

The children of St John's, Forfar have very kindly sent us 12s and Sir John Holden has sent a delicious box of oranges.

29th

We are very grateful to an anonymous donor from Edinburgh who kindly sent a roll of dress material.

The British surrendered at Kut later in the month, some 13,000 men taken prisoners and 2,500 sick soldiers released by the Turks. Some 4800 died due to disease, illness and neglect in the weeks that followed.

From the Warden

Easter Thoughts

The usual brightness of Easter was a little dimmed this year by an outbreak of influenza among the children. On Easter Day, we had about 40 children in bed and a day or two later we reached nearly 100, then it abated as suddenly as it appeared. None of the cases were serious and each meant three or four days in bed.

In spite of this the Festival was really bright and happy.

Easter is soon followed by "going away time" and during the first week in May about 40 boys and girls will be leaving the old roof to begin the battle of life. We shall miss them and we hope they will all prove worthy sons and daughters of Aberlour.

May 1916

1st May

This has been an exciting and busy day; no less than 20 boys and girls have left us to meet the stern realities of life. We never sent out so many in one day before, but we kept them back so that they might have their Easter holidays before starting work; and their employers were clamouring for them so we could keep them no longer. May God's richest blessing go with them all!

Three little people arrived in the evening; a clergyman brought one of them and is already enthusiastic about the Orphanage. He says he would like to stay here!

2nd

Two huge bundles this morning excited our curiosity and anticipations; they proved to contain about 100 yards of most beautiful cloth for boys' suits.

We are delighted indeed and most grateful!

3ʳᵈ

From St John's, Forres, comes a welcome sum of £22 collected during Lent.

4ᵗʰ

The usual half-yearly gift of garments from the Aberlour Orphanage Guild at Arbroath and from its Carnoustie Branch has arrived, and is a splendid addition to our store.

8ᵗʰ

Two truly magnificent bales have arrived from members of the Edinburgh Cathedral Work Party. They contain no less than 1069 garments for the children. This beats all records even for St Mary's, Edinburgh. It is particularly wonderful coming at such a time as this. We cannot do more than tender our deepest gratitude to all these good friends and assure them of our warmest appreciation of their work and labour of love.

British and French with the agreement of Russia signed convention for plans for the dismemberment of the Turkish Empire after an allied victory.

15ᵗʰ

We are grateful to the children of St Margaret's Orphanage, East Grinstead for a most generous gift of £1 18s.

The Chinese government agreed to supply France with 200,000 labourers to support its war effort.

From Lance Corporal Pritchard - 1/6 Seaforth Highlanders

I hope you are all well. We are at present in the trenches and are having a quiet time but at the end of last month we were knocked about a bit, the enemy having blown up 5 mines below our battalion. I assure you our boys stuck to their posts and fought hand to hand with the Huns. The earth shook and rocked as if it had been an earthquake, and the artillery from both sides were pouring in their death dealing missiles; the machine guns were rattling and clubs were swinging right and left. Our casualty list was heavy but by all accounts, the Germans suffered more.

We are having lovely weather and the country behind the lines is looking lovely with its growing crops.

I am sure that you will be preparing for the Sale. I wish I could be with you to assist Mr Robinson.

I met William Morrison the other day at an advanced medical post. We were chatting as strangers for a considerable time, when I asked him if he was ever at Aberlour Orphanage. I then found he was a brother of Albert who used to work in an office in London.

Kindest remembrances to all.

17th

Very many thanks to Mrs Anderson for her most kind subscription and for an extra gift of £1 which we have put to the Coal fund; what with cooking, laundry work and baths there is always a run on our coal cellar.

U S President Woodrow Wyatt announced that the US might have to intervene in the war and should have a role in any peace-making process.

22nd

Many thanks to John Maloney for 2s for the Former Inmates' Bed. Joseph Lang who left us only a few weeks ago, has sent us 5s for the coal fund.

23rd

Miss E. Scott Moncrieff kindly sends 5s for the summer treat with news of two of our girls in service.

From Private John Black - 1st Seaforths - Indian Expeditionary Force

I take this opportunity to let you know we have arrived in Mesopotamia. I have made a diary of our voyage from Cromarty to the banks of the Tigris, and it is very interesting reading.

If I were on holiday and coming to the old Home, I could give you a good lecture but it is a pity I am bashful.

I have a few curios for the Museum but as I am 8000 miles away and I am afraid that you will have to wait till I bring them. I have made notes of Malta, Port Said, Gibraltar, Alexandria, Aden and Basra and the scenery of the Suez Canal and the banks of the Tigris.

Before we left the ship we were all vaccinated and then we were allowed to go ashore. We cooked all our own food and I can assure that some of us would make very good cooks. Our daily rations consisted of bread, jam, bacon, cheese, beef, potatoes, onions, eggs and dates. We were considered to be well off, and there is no doubt about it. There are beautifully built houses and a large number of troops on each side of the canal; it is said to be 80 to 90 miles long. It took our troopship 17 hours to pass through.

There are a large number of troops out here in addition to the Seaforths and people of different nationalities. The Turks and the Arabs are to all outward appearance harmless but for all that I would not trust them further than I could throw them. I do not know what they would do if they got one of us in a quiet corner, but we are always on the alert in case of any disturbance. If I am here much longer I am afraid that I shall never speak English again.

I have not come across any of the old boys. It does not matter where they are so long as they are on active service.

I am sure that those of us who are spared to come through this awful war will be glad to have a reunion at the old Home and relate our experiences. If I am cut down, be assured I have died an honourable death. Best wishes to all. Farewell.

John's letter appeared in the May 1916 Magazine and in the next Magazine dated June 1916, Private William Morrison wrote from Mesopotamia to give the Orphanage the sad news of John Black's death. He was killed during the last attack of the Seaforths trying to relieve Kut. "He was well liked by his comrades in the regiment, and his chum said he never wished to meet a more kind-hearted fellow"

25th

Many thanks to H.C. for a useful gift of 12 pairs of socks and 2s for the summer treat.

26th

Her Royal Highness the Princess Royal has again kindly sent us her annual subscription of £5 for which we are exceedingly grateful.

26th

This is the Warden's birthday: as usual it is a holiday from school. We had a birthday feast, pennies and a cricket match and a bright warm summer's day.

27th

Today has brought a most valuable gift of £50. It is the third year we have received it and are most grateful to the generous donor who insists on remaining anonymous.

29th

This is the first day of another Sale and a wonderful Sale it is proving.

30th

Another sale has come and gone and a great success it has been. In a day and a half, we took over £263, which beats all records for a May Sale.

The British Home Fleet put to sea to intercept a major sortie by the German fleet. The Home Fleet sailed from Scapa Flow and Invergordon. Strong force of Battle Cruisers sailed from Rosyth, led by Sir David Beatty.

The Battle of Jutland started on 31st May and raged for a day. British Fleet suffered considerable losses and damage to ships. Admiral Beatty had to order his ships to retreat after suffering severe damage to several boats with one, The Indefatigable, disappearing in a massive explosion.

June 1916

1st

Very many thanks to the 8th Dundee (Episcopal Church) Company Boys' Brigade for a most welcome contribution of 10s to our funds.

German attack against the Ypres salient made initial progress but many of their gains were lost due to Canadian counterattacks.

Major Russian and British attacks were mounted to relieve the pressure on the French at Verdun. The battle continued into September.

5th

Many thanks to "A Friend, London" for 20 pairs of black stockings.

French and British declared a state of siege of Salonika and removed all the pro-German/Greek Officials.

7th

Mrs Johnston, the grandmother of one of our old boys, has very kindly sent us a Whitsuntide offering of 10s which we very much appreciate.

From Corporal Albert Morrison - 8th Royal Fusiliers France

It seems ages since I wrote last, and I scarcely know where to begin.

The first and most interesting incident to report is that I have been on leave to Aberdeen. We had spent three wretched nights within yards of the Germans and had just been relieved when the sergeant came along.

"Corporal Morrison, you will report yourself for fatigue at 2 o'clock" I had the usual grouse, and was just having something to eat before going on fatigue, when the sergeant major revealed himself, "Corporal Morrison you will report yourself to the Company Office to proceed on leave". There was no "grousing" on that order, but I could scarcely contain myself with excitement. In the short time at my disposal I cleaned myself as well as possible and as a canteen lid full of water would allow, and at 4 p.m. duly reported myself. My lucky star must have been in the ascendant for just as I was leaving the trenches, the Germans sprung a mine and the fatigue party had a rather warm time.

It was funny how, as we neared civilisation (represented by England) the means of travel improved.

After leaving the station we travelled by French train in which we were packed like sardines. It took us 6 hours to get to Boulogne and we were not sorry to get out and stretch our legs. As there were German submarines in the Channel, we hung about Boulogne till 2 in the afternoon. It was the same afternoon as the Sussex was torpedoed.

Back in London it was strange to be made a fuss of. One gentleman old enough to be my grandfather insisted upon me having his seat. As it was raining all the time we were in the trenches my uniform was in a pretty pickle, and everyone stared but one intelligent individual asked me whether I had come from the trenches.

Photo from National Library of Scotland's WW1 Collections.

Tea was brought to us in the carriages at various stops.

From the trenches to Aberdeen took about 45 hours. As you know the chief trouble out here is the nerves and as we had had a respectable dose of mines I was far from being steady, so decided to have a quiet time. In spite of having no rest for over a week, the first time I went to bed I found it impossible to sleep, bed itself was so strange. It was my full intention to come to Aberlour but I was so knocked up and the time was so short I had reluctantly to give up the idea.

On returning to my battalion, things were pretty rough. At present we are resting getting ready for the coming push.

My thoughts were with you all at Easter. On Easter Sunday we were in the trenches and it was very difficult that day to believe that we, in preparing death for others, were fighting for Christianity.

With love and all good wishes

Lord Kitchener was killed when the British Cruiser Hampshire was sunk by a German submarine making its way to Russia.

13th

Mr George Dalziel has sent a generous donation of £10 towards defraying the expenses of a summer treat, of which he is strongly of the opinion that the children should not be deprived.

We had a very pleasant visit from an old boy James Cardno, whom we had not seen for two years. He left donations to the Former Inmates' Bed. Another old boy, James Garden who was here on Sunday has also kindly given 10s to the Former Inmates' Bed.

15th

The children of the Sunday School, Peterhead have sent us the generous sum of £8, at their own express wish this is a larger contribution than usual in these anxious times, and we are very grateful for their kind gift and thought.

17th

Amy Haddrell kindly sends 3s for the Former Inmates' Bed and Private James Mclennan who has appeared for the first time in Khaki, has given 5s.

19th

Mr Culross sends us the handsome sum of £23 towards the Printers' Beds annually supported by the staff of McCorquodale and Company. This is a particularly handsome gift considering that the staff have been heavily depleted by the War.

From Private William Robertson - 3rd Seaforths Mesopotamia

I thank you very much for the magazine – it took nearly six weeks to come from Aberlour.

I was grieved to read of the death of Robert McNeilly. We were great chums in Cromarty when we were undergoing our training.

I am now on the Divisional staff, the Rev R Irwin is my master. He is the Church of England Chaplain. I am sorry to say he was wounded about a month ago. We attacked the Turks and drove them back 10 miles. The rifle fire of the Turks was something awful. I considered myself lucky to come out of the fight without a scratch.

The weather is very hot. Our worst enemies are the heat and the flies.

We are quite close to the River Tigris, and goodness only knows what we should do without it, as we are drinking water all day long. The heat is so intense that the sweat pours down your face, as if someone had poured a bucket of water over your head.

I suppose the flowers and the trees are looking their best at the Orphanage now. Here we have nothing but sandy desert.

I have very sad news to tell you of John Black. I was stung in the eye by some insect and was in the same hospital as another Seaforth and asked him if he knew John Black. He said he did and that he was killed at the last attack when the Seaforths tried to relieve Kut. It made me sick to hear it. I was looking forward to giving him a surprise when we met. He was well liked by his comrades in the regiment, and his chum said he never wished to meet a more kind-hearted fellow. I would be very pleased to hear from you- even a few lines would cheer me up in this dreary land. Best love to all.

20th

Miss Fraser, Pitlochry, has sent most acceptable gifts of stockings, caps and scarves, which were knitted by her maid, Agnes Butchard, at odd moments.

The British began their bombardment of the German trenches on the Somme. Around 1.7 million British shells were fired on the first day though a third of the shells failed to explode.

30th

The children have today begun their summer holidays for six weeks. It is a very wet day, but we hope for better in the future.

From Driver David McKenzie - Egyptian Expeditionary Force

I am in the middle of the desert trying to keep the Turks back, but have not forgotten the "Old Home" although I am so far away. The heat is dreadful. It is too bad to send the "hardy Scots" here. We get under cover from 12 to 4 o'clock, owing to the torrid conditions.

We are allowed 4 pints of water a day. That has to do for washing our clothes, faces and shaving. You can call it water if you like. The heat has it nearly boiled before we get it.

I hear John Black is in Mesopotamia. I wish I could meet him and some of the other old boys.

Be sure and write a long letter soon, as I long to hear about the "Old Home" Are there any signs of the war ending? We know nothing here.

Kindest remembrances to all.

July 1916

The whole magazine was taken up with the report of the Annual Meeting held on July 27th 1916.

We include some short excerpts.

Sadly, there were no letters from "old Boys" published that month.

July was a significant month in WW1 with major losses and disasters in many areas of the war.

July saw the offensive of the British on the Somme start on an intensely hot day. 224,000 shells had been fired every hour and shortly before the advance began 10 huge underground mines were exploded beneath the German trenches burying many of the German troops.

Early gains were made near Albert but further north the situation was disastrous. Infantry were faced with uncut barbed wire, and carrying excessive equipment the troops were faced by a wall of machine gun fire.

At the end of the day there were 57,000 casualties of whom 19,000 were killed. German losses were estimated at 8,000.

There were serious difficulties in getting reinforcements to the frontlines to relieve the exhausted survivors.

Lloyd George became Secretary of War following the death of Lord Kitchener.

The Annual General Meeting

The Bishop of Moray in moving the reports said

"Notwithstanding the circumstances of the time, and irrespective of the many calls on the pockets of the charitable, it is very satisfactory that a positive financial report has been presented." He thought that people were learning that whatever they must economise in, they must not economise in their charities.

He spoke of the dedication of the staff and the way in which they carried on the traditions and care of the founder, Canon Jupp.

He also said that it was almost a miracle that it was possible the children could be clothed at 16s per annum- about the price of a pair of boots- and it could not be done without the ladies of the many Work Parties who sent garments for the children.

The Bishop also spoke about the gratitude that so many boys were serving their country voluntarily. He knew of no institution with a better record. He hoped that all who remembered the Orphanage in their prayers remembered the children living there and those who had gone out from it especially those fighting for their country.

The Warden spoke in highly complementary terms of the great assistance he had received from his staff, making special mention of The Sub-Warden, Mr Kissack, Mr White, Treasurer and Miss Wilson whose services in looking after the working girls was invaluable.

Manager's Report for 1915-6

The average number of children on the Register was 486; during the year 97 were admitted and 83 left. Farmers continue to testify their appreciation of the boys whom they engage. We have also received very satisfactory accounts of the girls who have gone to service. The Orphanage will always have reason to be proud of the noble response of its old boys to their country's call. We have already heard of 20 killed in the war and doubtless others have fallen.

Our Isolation Hospital is still given up to the work of the VAD Red Cross Society.

Our half yearly sales are well supported and it was reported that the May 1916 Sale was the best May Sale on record making £263 in a day and a half.

The manager also expressed the trust that the Orphanage had in the good hand of God, each year we have more abundant proof of his faithfulness. It will be so again this year: we are still in the midst of this terrible war: expenses will increase: many private incomes will be reduced: and yet these 500 children will continue to be fed, warmed and clothed.

August 1916

3rd

A party of boys had a fine excursion today to the top of Ben Rinnes and immensely enjoyed themselves; it was a good day for the purpose, bright and not too hot, but a trifle windy. They are very pleased with themselves for having accomplished the climb.

Miss Dundas very kindly sends £1 for the Coal Fund for which we return thanks.

The children all had a special tea today, the gift of a kind neighbour, and they have much appreciated it.

The British offensive on the Somme was a month old and casualties totalled 158,000 plus 40,000 elsewhere on the Western Front. German casualties totalled 160,000.

The Turks attacked a British held rail junction near the Suez Canal. British forces were assisted by New Zealand troops.

7th

Miss E. Fowler Jones sends £3 more for the Yorkshire Bed: part of it is the proceeds of the sale of a large crochet cloth which she had made. Many thanks and congratulations.

Our heartiest congratulations to Albert Morrison: last week we had two letters from him: in the first he told us that he had been awarded the Military Medal.

From Sergeant Albert Morrison - Royal Fusiliers – France

I am pleased to inform you that I have been awarded the Military Medal. We were in action on 7th July and our brigade did some fine work, which more than pleased our General. I am not altogether sure that I deserve this medal, because everyone did splendidly, and the odds against us were heavy, but all our officers were "hors de combat" at a very early stage and also the NCOs senior to me, so I was in charge of what was left of my company.

Marching back after we had been relieved, our divisional band met us and struck up our march past "The British Grenadiers". One feels pride of regiment when marching to our march past; but on this occasion we looked at our depleted ranks and thought of our comrades who failed to answer the roll call. Everyone was affected. My company officer was wounded before the action, but insisted on coming over with us. He was killed whilst rallying the company.

Ourselves we absolutely did the impossible, and although we cleared the way for those who have followed us and by taking the position have been instrumental in saving countless lives.

Imagine 40 foot dugouts which no shells can shatter, countless machine guns – you have an impregnable position. We took it. Our Colonel was mortally wounded and died subsequently. His last message was "Tell Major---- to give my love to the boys- they are a brave lot of men. Tell Captain M---- from me that the artillery has been very, very excellent, and words cannot express what the infantry think of them."

Albert wrote a further letter on 11th August

Many thanks for your letter. We have been in action again and I was slightly wounded on the 3rd August.

We were attacked around 11p.m. The artillery prepared the way. We were just beginning to find our own shells troublesome when the fire ceased. That was our signal to charge so with a mighty yell we dashed forward and hey presto the trench was ours. When I reached the trench I started sending up star shells in the hope of catching any of the enemy running away. As I was sending one up, a soldier entering the trench jumped on me, and I caught the full kick of the flare pistol on the forehead. The blow stunned me, but I did not consider it bad enough for me to leave the trench. I went the next morning to have the wound dressed, meaning to return at once. The doctors would not hear of it, but I had a few words with them and told them my part in the business was the fighting. I went out, but when I got to the trench I collapsed, and had to be carried to the motor ambulance. I am all right again.

Photo from National Library of Scotland's WW1 Collections.

Yesterday we had the signal honour of being inspected by his Majesty the King. The Prince of Wales was also present, and all distinguished guests.

I send my best wishes to everyone and trust you are all well.

10th

Many thanks to Miss Clarke of Avenel and members of the Guild at Melrose for their very excellent parcel of garments.

16th

One friend who contributed had been at Aberlour many years ago and spent such a happy time there that she called her house in Dublin, "Aberlour".

17th

Mrs Henry Tod, Roslin had greatly gladdened our hearts by sending a splendid parcel of shirts for our older boys. They have supplied a long felt want.

From John R Elliott (Smith) HMS Queen

I am writing to let you know how I have been getting on since I left the Old Home.

Willie and I both enlisted together on June 9th last year, when we were sent to the R.N Barracks at Shotley. After undergoing a course on seamanship and schoolwork lasting 3 months, we had to sit for an examination to see if we could qualify for the advanced class, wireless telegraphy. I qualified for the advanced class getting an average percentage on all subjects of 90 %, thanks to the schooling I had with you.

I then had another course of gunnery, trigonometry, mechanics, electricity and navigation. I soon picked up these new subjects.

Willie qualified for wireless telegraphy and went through a course of Morse and electricity. I went to sea a few weeks before him and he is now aboard the Benbow.

I am a good distance away from home now, and the heat here is something awful; we do nothing but sweat from first thing in the morning to the last thing at night, then on to the morning again. So you will see we are having a fine high old time. We have voluntary bathing twice a day, and that helps us keep a bit cooler, but not for long.

How are all the boys getting on? Would you please let me know when you write how some of the old boys I used to know are doing?

How is Mr Robinson getting on with the Choir, and do you still have the annual play?

Mr White used to say that I was growing pretty fast, I wonder what he would say if he saw me now!

Give my kindest regards to all.

German High Seas Fleet launched a major attack against Britain but an attack on Sunderland thwarted by intelligence gatherers, allowed the British Fleet to sail and counter the attack.

Two British Cruisers were sunk by German submarines and led to the British breaking off their confrontation on the High Seas.

22nd

The children returned to school today, after spending seven weeks of most enjoyable holiday. With the exception of a few wet days at the beginning of the holiday the weather was beautifully fine. The time passed quickly with cricket matches, and frequent long walks in our lovely country. The swimming pond was in great requisition, and 27 managed to swim round it. This is the ambition of all the bathers. We know of two of our old boys who saved their lives by being able to swim when wrecked. They had both learned this desirable art in our pond.

27th

Mr Harding has greatly relieved our minds by sending the handsome donation of £20 for the Coal Fund. Not only is the price of coal rising daily but we find difficulty in obtaining a supply. Owing to Mr Harding's kind gift we have ordered an extra quantity at once.

Italy declared war on Germany.

Sixteen German airships attacked London and South East England. The results were poor due to bad weather and technical problems.

September 1916

2nd

We were very pleased to have a visit today from two old boys, Patrick Hamilton and William Grant; they each kindly gave 10s towards the Former Inmates' Bed.

From Private Ernest Partridge 7th Camerons, France.

I am writing to let you know I have had my first experience of the trenches in France and I can assure you I know now what it is like to be under shell fire. I was very excited at first but I soon settled down. I was standing next my Company Officer all the time the shelling was going on. If it had not been for his encouragement I think I would have had shell shock. He is an excellent Officer for his men, and every one of us would do everything in our power for him.

I have met a good many old boys out here. I met Peter Banks in a trench and we spoke about what we would do after the war was over, if we are spared. I also met David Pearson, he is in the 6th Camerons, and Donald Francis is in the same regiment. They are both well and happy.

We made an advance on 15th September. I am sorry to tell you that Robert Dunbar was wounded on that day. He was hit in the face by a fragment of shell. I shall miss him very much as he was my best chum.

I am collecting interesting things from the battlefield and I am sure that Mr White would like some for the Museum. I am always thinking of you.

General Sir Douglas Haig agreed to another major renewal of the Somme offensive which had degenerated into a series of localised battles.

The British with French support secured all of the German second-line defences which had been expected to fall in the opening stages of the Battle of the Somme.

4th

We had a short visit from Maggie Milne, who is in service not very far away, and who kindly gave 5s 6d to the Former Inmates' Bed.

8th

Two very useful presents are 25 pairs of boys' stockings from Miss Donald of Elgin and some jam from Mrs Scott of Laggan, Carron.

We are very grieved to learn that three more of our old boys, Robert Brown, Edwin McCulloch and John Johnston have been killed in the war. The first named is a brother of Alexander Brown who fell many months ago. R.I.P

From Private Harry Gould - Indian Expeditionary Force

I am writing to let you know that I have been sent to a hospital in Bombay suffering from heat stroke and enteric fever. I received the magazine today for which I thank you.

You have no idea how the magazine cheered me up.

I notice the letter from John Black in the Indian Expeditionary Force –I remember him and must try to find him. I hope that he managed to survive our last attack against the Turks. The heat was dreadful; it was often 120° in the shade.

I am very pleased to see that so many of the old boys have joined the army. I am sure that you must be proud of them. I am sorry to note that so many have been killed. When I read over the names it brings back to my memory the good old times we used to have.

As regards myself I am much better. I think I will be sent to some hill station in India, until I get stronger. I trust you are all well.

Is Lachlan McDonald still with you? It seems ages since I worked with him in the gardens.

Please convey my best wishes to all in the old Home.

14th

The weather has turned decidedly cold: there was snow only three miles up the country this morning, and fires would have been acceptable, but we dare not start them yet, because of the bills.

From Private Peter Banks 8th Seaforths in France

I received the magazine a few days ago and had the greatest pleasure

in reading all about the year's work. I hope you are having good weather. Here it has been wonderfully fine. We are now in the wilderness as all the villages we pass through are in ruins. No one would know that a village existed, until you get close up to it and then you only see a heap of bricks.

We passed Cecil's Battalion (Benjamin Pritchard was also called Cecil) about a fortnight ago but it was very early and did not get a chance to see him. I heard from a soldier in the 2nd Battalion that George Aberdein had come through the big push all right. I was talking to Matthew Jack and he got buried by a shell along with four others but he is on duty again.

Kindly remember me to all.

British launched offensive known as Fleur-Courcelette, tanks appeared on the Western Front for the first time.

Many tanks were knocked out or became stuck in the mud and many suffered mechanical failure. General Haig requested a further 1000 tanks to be built for the Front.

19th

We are most grateful to an anonymous donor for a grand roll of flannel from Edinburgh: also to Mrs Scott for another good gift of 40 lbs of jam.

From Private Colin Hay - Manchester Regiment

It is quite a long time since I wrote to you but I am sure you will excuse me when you know that I have been wounded, and have been in hospital for more than a month. I was helping to erect barbed wire entanglements in "No Man's Land". The next platoon to mine did not know we were out, so a listening post fired two volleys at us. We were three in number, but I was the only one wounded. I got two bullets in the left leg, just above the knee, three smaller pieces in the calf and another piece in my left forearm. I think it was quite a nice collection of scrap iron. It will keep me out of fighting for some time. I am not sorry, for I assure you words cannot describe what we have to go through at the Front. I sincerely hope you are all well.

Photo from National Library of Scotland's WW1 Collections.

21st

We much appreciate a nice box of garments from Miss McIntyre and her class of girls in the Sunday School of All Saints, St Andrews.

Further attacks spearheaded by 13 tanks succeeded in capturing the village of Thriepval. Some British gains were made but progress was slow because of strong German resistance and the mud.

24th

Mr McCorquodale has sent us a fine box of Spey salmon, sufficient for all staff, which will be much enjoyed.

From Private George Partridge - 3rd Battalion Seaforths, Cromarty.

I arrived quite safely on Wednesday evening. I am sorry that I did not write sooner, but I felt quite homesick after being on furlough. I was sorry leaving the Home, for I thought that it might be the last time I should ever visit it, but I will keep my spirits up in the hope that I shall see you all again.

I have not heard from my brother Ernest, who is in France. I trust he will manage to come safely through the severe fighting. I send my best wishes to all.

Our bill for coals last year amounted to £630 which was the highest on record. At the end of September, the Fund has donations of £68.

October 1916

1st

We were very pleased to see Mrs McDougall (Mary Cameron) who brought her husband to see her old home. She had not been for twelve years, and there were many threads to pick up and many things to talk about concerning the old days.

3rd

We experienced this morning the first frost of the season and a Christmas gift follows appropriately.

From Private William Robertson – c/o Chaplain, Mesopotamian Expeditionary Force

I received your most kind and welcome letter at the beginning of the week. I am glad to see that you are all keeping well in the dear old home, but I am sure you will be having a lot of worry, and I do hope this awful war will soon end and that the world may be at peace and happiness again.

The weather here is still very hot; the average temperature is from 107 to 112° in the shade. In the middle of July it was 115 to 122° in the shade so you see we have been nearly roasted alive. There is nothing doing out here at the present moment apart for our artillery firing a few rounds now and then.

I am sorry that I did not see John Black before he went into action; I was told by some fellows that he was round my company asking for me but as ill luck would have it I was not there. When the regiment came out of action I enquired about him again and it was then I received the sad news of his death. Frank Bain has not re-joined the regiment again yet, and if he is not disabled I do not suppose it will be long before I see him again.

This week has been full of surprises for me, and I could hardly believe my eyes when I received a letter from my old master, Mr Black of Achnahannet. He was telling me men have been very scarce lately and that he had some trouble before he could get down his crops. The boys would enjoy their bathes out here, and you would take a long time to get them out of the water again

In the evening while I am having my usual dip in the Tigris I often think of the gay old times that I used to have in the bathing pond, the only thing that is needed out here is the whistle and the barking of Luke.

(Luke was one of Canon Jenks' dogs and his barking signalled that the children should leave the pond!)

Now that summer holidays are over I hope that the children have had such splendid weather that they have not missed their picnics.

It is nearing my birthday, and I am afraid that there will be no holiday for me this year.

With best love and good wishes to all.

5th

We have received a most handsome gift of £18 from Mrs Russell, Milnathort for the Coal Fund: this is valuable help indeed to our heavy bills, and we are truly grateful.

German authorities agreed to resume attacks on merchant ships, irrespective of their nationality, although it was specifically forbidden for submarine commanders to torpedo ships without warning them first.

6th

A splendid gift of girls' dress material has arrived this morning from Mrs St Quinton; it is just what we needed, and nothing could have been more welcome or opportune.

7th

The father of one of our boys has sent us a voluntary donation of 10s in addition to the sum he pays regularly for the boy's donation and we much appreciate the gift.

Atlantic - German Submarine sank three British, one Dutch and one Norwegian vessels off the East Coast of the United States.

11th

Four great sacks of garments have arrived this morning from Miss Macdonald and the members of the Aberlour Orphanage Guild, representing their half-year's labour on our behalf. It is a great and valuable gift, worthy of the reputation of the Guild, and proves once again that there is no diminution in their interest through the pressures of other urgent claims. We offer our sincerest gratitude to every one of the contributors.

13th

We have received a most valuable gift of a cheque for £30 and a parcel of excellent shirts, dresses and jerseys, and are deeply grateful to the anonymous donor, who always wishes to remain anonymous.

Middle East

Captain T.E. Lawrence arrived in Jeddah to try to liaise between British establishment and leaders of the Arab revolt. Lawrence was an advocate for an Independent Arab State.

16th

Mr George Dalziel send us a very handsome gift of £15 for the Coal Fund and says "The bairns must be kept warm this winter".

We have also most gratefully received two gifts in kind: a fine stag from his Grace the Duke of Richmond and Gordon and 40 rabbits from Mr Barclay. These are most valuable and acceptable.

21st

We deeply regret to learn this morning that another of our old boys, Robert Webster, has fallen in the war: he was killed on September 26th. This makes the 27th death that we know of.

The French launched a counterattack to capture the territory to the North East of Verdun. Under cover of mist the French take 6000 German prisoners.

25th

Six little people have arrived today from a long distance- Leytonstone- whose father fell victim of one of the air raids last year. Will anyone support one or more of these children? They seem very bright.

27th

From far away Malay, The Rev E.L. Dawson sends us £5 contributed by the Sunday scholars of St Mark's, Serebam. We are very glad to feel that the children take a real interest in our Home.

November 1916

1st

The children are thoroughly enjoying their All Saints' holiday in bright sunshiny weather.

French Commander in Chief, General Joffre outlined plans to General Sir Douglas Haig for an Anglo-French offensive on the Western Front of France.

2nd

We have received a most valuable present of 10 dozen eggs from Mrs Harding , Wester Elchies; and also an outfit from the Misses Gordon Duff for the little girl they clothe from year to year. Very many thanks.

"An offering from the Scholars of St Andrew's Catechism Class, Banff" consists of apples, grapes and toys from their Harvest Thanksgiving- a most acceptable present.

4th

Another grand present of 12 dozen eggs from Mrs Harding! And "eggs is eggs" in these days!

Photo from National Library of Scotland's WW1 Collections.

6th

Harry Handforth, just arrived from Canada to fight for his old country, was on his way to pay us a visit when he was recalled to his regiment; we are much disappointed at not seeing him, and are very grateful for the £1 he sent for the Former Inmates' Bed.

Lady Beatty has asked us to take a little girl whose father was killed in the Jutland Battle, and we will gladly do so.

From Private William Brown 4/5th Black Watch

I am writing to let you know that I have been wounded, and am now lying in a London Hospital. We were in a stiff fight on the 25th October and I was then put out of action. I lay in the open for three days and all that time my wounds were not dressed, and I had nothing to eat or drink. I was unable to crawl in, as my wounds were too severe. On the Tuesday night a number of men were on their way to bomb the Germans, in fact they were a raiding party. As they were returning I called to them and the Officer in Charge said he would send two men for me. He did so on Wednesday evening and I can assure you I was grateful to him. The men carried me to a dug out and I was gasping for a drink. The good men soon made me a cup of hot tea which revived me greatly. On Thursday I was conveyed to the first-aid dressing station. I have to undergo an operation to get a piece of gas shell out of my leg.

I got five pieces out of my back, which is almost better, but I am afraid it will be a long time before my leg is well. [*William had already lost two of his brothers who were killed earlier in the War*]

I hope you will write soon and let me know how you are all keeping in the old Home. Best wishes to everyone

9th

Mrs Smith Shand very kindly sends us a bundle of *The Graphic*, and is going to send this paper regularly, which will be much appreciated.

11th

A valuable gift of 36 stockings has been sent by Mrs Montgomery from Birnam and Dunkeld Stocking Guild.

British Fifth Army initiated the Battle of Ancre to the north east of Albert. The village of Beaumont Hamel fell to the British. Fighting continued to mid-November. This battle effectively concluded the British Offensive on the Somme. British casualties were enormous; some 420,000 men. French casualties numbered 205,000 troops and the Germans 500,000.

14th

Mrs Clarke sends us a valuable gift of 20 yards of flannel. We are very grateful for this as we were entirely out of flannel and did not know how we were going to rig the boys out with drawers this winter. Fortunately the weather has been keeping mild lately.

16th

An old boy, John Maloney, has thoughtfully sent us a present of clothes.

The British had by the end of the offensive still not captured some of their first day objectives. France launched a final offensive in Verdun and regained much of the territory lost to the German forces in the north-east of Verdun. French troops gained success by using a creeping barrage where troops advance behind a wall of artillery fire.

18th

We have received many welcome contributions today for which we are sincerely grateful. Coals and Christmas money, a fine roe deer from Sir George MacPherson Grant and some excellent socks for elder lads made and sent by Mr D. Young, Kirriemuir!

19th

The children today have much enjoyed a barrel of apples most kindly sent by Mrs Shand Smith. They were grand apples and have given much pleasure on a wet Sunday afternoon.

22nd

The father of two of our boys has kindly sent 10s in addition to the maintenance for the boys for the Coal Fund. Another father of two girls writes, "Words fail to express my gratitude for all the care my children are getting: they look so well and so happy".

24th

We are very grateful to L.S. for a welcome donation of £2 and for the kind offer to send a parcel to an old boy at the Front. We have gladly given her a name and address.

From Private James McLennan 12th Company Black Watch, France

I am sure you will get a surprise when you open this letter. I am quite well and I sincerely hope that you, the matrons, and all the children are enjoying good health.

I thank you very much for the Magazine. I see by the last number that several more of the old boys have been killed or wounded. I was particularly sorry to notice the death of John Black. He was a very nice fellow and a favourite with everyone.

I have been under shell fire two or three times but not so badly as the poor lads in the trenches. I have travelled through France and some parts of Belgium but so far have not seen any of the Aberlour boys.

I am enjoying myself here. We are road making, and are in a very quiet place. We cannot hear the sound of guns as we did the first two months. The first time I heard the guns at night I could not close my eyes. Now I sleep so soundly that I do not think a cartload of stones thrown against the door would waken me.

I have seen more than a thousand German prisoners. Some of them are very fine looking fellows. And many are quite young. I spoke to one a short time ago and he told me he was in the first line of the trenches the day before he was taken prisoner. He was very glad to be captured, and he wished the war over; and so say all of us but I am afraid it will be many months yet.

I had a letter from my late master at Forres. He told me that he had only three men on the farm instead of eight, but they had managed to get through with the harvest. I trust you had good crops. Kindly remember me to everyone in the Old Home. I think of you all every day.

25th

Mrs Mackenzie Murray has kindly sent a dozen scrapbooks with a lot of pictures to be cut and pasted in, which will give fine occupation and pleasure in the long winter evenings.

Long range German bombers launched their first daylight raid on London, one plane dropped six small bombs on the centre of London wounding 10 civilians.

28th

This has been a very busy and very successful day, the first day of our sale; the full results will not be known till tomorrow. We have 32 old boys sleeping here to-night and three others during the day. It is very gratifying to see them coming in such numbers, and all so well and in such good spirits.

The visits of the "farmers", *(most of the boys who came would be working on farms nearby)* cause no little excitement among the younger generation, all anxious to hear the experiences of their former companions and to see what treasures and goodies there may be for distribution. A bit of excitement at times does us all good. But it is back to work tomorrow. Holidays are few and short when schooldays are done.

Admiral Sir David Beatty was appointed to command the Home Fleet in place of Admiral Sir John Jellicoe.

Our Sale

Another Jumble Sale has passed and it is with very grateful hearts that we are able to say it was a wonderful success.

In the day and a half of the Sale we took no less than £255.

Many years ago we heard our Founder say that the Sales must begin to fall off but over the years since the first Sale in 1885 they have made £11,835 – an amazing total.

Note from the Warden

We are very grateful to the many friends who sent parcels and papers to the boys whose addresses we gave last month. The recipients wish us to tender their sincerest thanks to the kind donors.

One wounded soldier writes: "I have simply been overwhelmed with the kindness since the issue of the Magazine".

A gentleman writes that he will remember our boys till they get to Berlin!

The Warden notes the injuries to William Brown and gives his address for any letters or parcels as the Military Hospital in Covent Garden, London.

December 1916

No letters from old boys were published in December but an account of Aberlour's Christmas was included in the Magazine.

1st

The last of our term visitors left us this morning, but another arrived in the evening, making forty-one old boys whom we have seen this week.

Mr G.F. McCorquodale has sent a handsome gift of £10 to provide Christmas fare for the children.

Two more old boys came tonight for Sunday, making forty-three in six days: we think this is easily a record.

5th

We were deeply grieved to hear today of the deaths of three more of our old boys, John Gardner, Peter Lawler and William Mackenzie. When will these horrors cease!

Lance Corporal Benjamin Pritchard sends us 7s 6d from the trenches for our Christmas dinner and wishes he could share it with us: so do we; and we appreciate his gift very much.

A Mr W. Ross on one of HM Trawlers, whose children were here for some time, sends 10s for Christmas with a very kind and grateful letter. May he be spared to spend Christmas 1917 in peace and happiness with his own family!

David Lloyd George replaced Herbert Asquith as Prime Minister.

7th

The Misses Tindal, Edinburgh, have kindly sent two specially good parcels containing 58 garments for our children's wear.

8th

Mary Grant aged 5 has again sent a splendid gift of Christmas crackers which will cause great fun and merriment. Our best thanks to the little donor.

11th

This is Founder's Day, the 86th anniversary of Canon Jupp's birth. The children are having a holiday from school as usual, and have enjoyed a barrel of apples, the usual kind gift of Miss Begbie, and various other pleasures.

12th

We are very grateful to Private William Morrison Grant (Canadian Contingent) who has been spending a few days leave with us, for a generous gift of £1 to the Former Inmates' Bed.

British offensive started along the Tigris River with 48,000 men, 170 artillery pieces and 24 aircraft and numerous armed river steamers. Heavy rain slowed the British Advance.

14th

We have received boxes and parcels of toys, games and books from three anonymous donors in Edinburgh. We tender our warmest thanks for all these gifts, which will help us much through the coming season.

On the Western Front at Verdun, enormous losses of 360,000 French troops and 336,000 German troops were recorded.

16th

We are very grateful to Mrs Wood for a most acceptable gift of 46 rabbits and 5 hares. They will provide a treat for the children, and will reduce our butcher's bill, which is always especially heavy this month.

19th

Mrs Purvis Russell Montgomery has sent £1 in lieu of sweeties and a most delightful parcel of books. This is a grand Christmas present, which will be much appreciated.

Lloyd George made a major speech, in rejecting peace proposals he said "We shall put our trust rather in an unbroken army than a broken faith".

20th

A very valuable present has come from Miss Rose in Nairn, in the shape of a large bottle of Cod Liver Oil Emulsion and another of Parrish's Chemical Food: we find these invaluable for delicate children or for those given to chilblains.

21st

We are deeply grateful to "Inasmuch" for a very handsome cheque for £45. This is indeed a Christmas Present to make our hearts glad.

Our neighbour Mr Grant has again sent his annual Christmas gift and a barrel of apples and a box of oranges: all these are gifts for which we are truly grateful and which we value much.

The children's Christmas holidays began at noon today: the ground is gloriously slippery, so a large number had a good afternoon of sliding; others began to make preparations for hanging the Christmas decorations; a few diligent ones scrubbed the large dining hall. *[The hall measured 85 feet by 33 feet!]*

23rd

Today has brought us a great gift in the form of a cheque for £350 to endow a bed in memory of a gallant soldier.

[This was from the parents of Lieutenant Valentine Don who died in the action at Loos, September 1915.] The Warden tendered the truest sympathy to his bereaved ones.

26th

Several of our neighbours have sent gifts: cake, footballs, oranges, turkeys. We are grateful indeed.

29th

The congregation of St Martin's, Gorgie Road, Edinburgh have kindly contributed £3 8s.

The prolonged battle on the Somme continued, General Haig said

the British have fought half of the German army and taken 38,000 prisoners.

In the month of December, German submarines were credited with sinking 167 vessels. Of this total 70 belonged to neutral countries.

CHRISTMAS 1916

Our doings at Christmas vary very little, but we like to give each year a short account, to bring the old scenes back to the minds of those who used to join in them but are now far away.

And if the doings are the same the spirit is always fresh: our family is ever young, and looks at Christmas with eyes that never grow up, and to which the festive signs never have time to lose their freshness. There are always some who are spending their first Christmas with us and always some their last. Even to the oldest of us Christmas retains its youthful fascination because of the youthful excitement that surges round us and carries us along: it is good that is so.

Christmas Eve was on Sunday; with the result we had a large congregation at the First Evensong, many from the village taking part in our beautiful and hearty service of joy. Thanks to the generosity of many friends; who in spite of the dark times seemed determined that our children should have brightness, the social part of the festival lost none of its time-honoured features.

The tables at breakfast groaned with sausages, baps, bread and butter and tea and at dinner under their load of beef, potatoes, plum pudding and oranges. The groaning soon ceased for the tables were soon cleared of their good things with the rapidity that springs from healthy appetites.

21 former inmates joined us for the dinner 17 boys and 4 girls. We missed our soldier boys of the last two years, but it was not their fault, and we did not fail to remind ourselves that they were absent because they were engaged in the stern business of defending our homes from the terrible fates of Belgium and Serbia. We made the rafters ring with cheers for them!

Tea, a meal of more modest dimensions was served about 5 o'clock, with the accompaniment of crackers, a source of great delight.

Then at 7 o'clock began the Christmas Dance. Scotsmen dance at every occasion except, we believe a funeral; and we danced well too.

The dancing went on merrily till eleven o'clock. We sang Auld Lang Syne and so closed a Christmas Day which brought unalloyed happiness to all and was described as "the best Christmas ever".

The little ones who were too young for the dance were entertained with a gorgeous Christmas tree and a gramophone.

We warmly thank everybody who contributed in any way to the day's happiness and wish all a bright New Year, with its end in days of peace.

January 1917

The year 1917 was dominated by the Russian Revolution which released German troops for service elsewhere and the declaration of war on Germany by the U.S.

Our financial year will end on the last day of February. In consequence of exorbitant prices of all kinds of food, our current account is at a dangerously low level, and we are afraid we will face a serious deficit.

1st January

We wish everyone a bright New Year with peace before its close.

The children are this evening enjoying the last dance of another Christmas season.

3rd

Two very valuable presents in kind received today are a hind from His Grace the Duke of Richmond and Gordon and a sheep from Mr Findlay of Aberlour, for which we are most grateful.

6th

No money at all today!

From Lance Corporal Benjamin Pritchard - 1/6th Seaforth Highlanders

I hope you will excuse me for not writing sooner, but I have been in hospital for a considerable time, and writing from there would have meant complaints about myself, and that is not very interesting.

When I returned to my regiment, I rejoined the doctor's staff.

I am sure that you followed the great advance which commenced on 13th November, and which proved to be a great success. [Battle of Ancre] The morning of the first stroke of battle, a heavy mist lay across the battlefield. Our men were ready to leap the trenches at a given signal, which was in the form of a great mine. When it exploded, the earth shook as if it had been an earthquake, and the artillery opened such a terrible fire that no living creature could live under it. As the curtain of fire moved forward the boys cleared the ground of the enemy either by bayonets or by prisoners.

After taking a number of trenches, their next work was to capture the village. Here our men ferreted out Fritz from his dugouts by bombing like a weasel after a rabbit.

After that great task they headed up the hill and when dusk set in our comrades had reached their objective. The casualties were rather heavy, but the enemy paid dearly for their resistance.

Our Brigade alone took 1500 prisoners. A Hun actually told me that the Germans no longer drink to "the day". The prisoners were employed to carry our wounded to the advanced dressing station.

I am sorry to add that three more old boys have fallen in this great struggle.

I hope the Sale was a great success. All eyes will now be turned to the Christmas Festival. I will send you a small donation to the expense of the dinner. I heartily wish I could be present, but perhaps next year, when we trust peace may reign on the earth once more.

7th

We are most grateful for the goodly sum of £4 5s so generously sent by the Sunday Scholars of St Salvador's, Dundee.

Middle East

British troops massed in Egypt to begin to clear the Turks out of the Sinai Peninsula prior to launching an invasion of Palestine.

9th

Good gifts received today for which we are very grateful are £5 for coals and 4 pairs of socks from Miss Haldane and two nice hinds from Mr Grant.

11th

Ethel Punshon, a former inmate from whom we had not heard since she left 18 years ago, has sent a generous gift of £1, half for the Former Inmates' Bed and half for the Coal Fund. It is nice to feel that the old Home is still kindly remembered after all these years.

12th

We have gratefully received a nice parcel of knitted garments, very kindly made by the children of Mr Wilson, the gardener at Buckromb.

From Private Matthew Jack - Artillery Regiment

I thank you very much for your letter, and also for the magazine. There is nothing I appreciate more than to get in touch with the Home of my Youth. I see that you have never had any word of James

Duncan being killed. He lost his life on the Somme by one of those terrible "whizz-bangs" He was attached to the Machine Gun Corps, and we are always beside them. I was having a nice talk with him the night before he was killed. Poor fellow, I shall miss him very much, as he was my best chum.

As I am writing this letter you will be busy selling at the November Sale. I hope the drawings will amount to a good sum, as I am sure you must find it a very hard task to "keep the home fires burning"

I am sorry to hear that four more boys have been killed. The Orphanage has paid its toll in this fight for liberty and I am sure that future generations will look with pride at its Roll of Honour.

Please remember me to Mr White, Mr Kissack, Mr Symons and Mr Robinson and all in the Home who know me. I hope you are having better weather than we are having. As I am writing it is raining heavily and the ground is in a terrible state. Best wishes to all.

18th

Our hearts were gladdened today by the gift of a splendid roll of flannel from our good friend, Mrs J.J. Johnstone. It is especially valuable in this cold weather.

US President Woodrow Wyatt called on all the combatant nations fighting World War 1 to agree "peace without victory". British and French rejected the proposal having found some of the German demands unacceptable.

23rd

Miss Wharton Duff sends a valuable gift of serge, flannel and flannelette, for which we are very grateful indeed.

From Private John McKay - Scottish Horse regiment

I have just received your most welcome letter, and I am so glad to know you are all well.

As for myself I am in the pink of condition, and am still going strong. At present we are having a spell in the trenches. I like trench life extraordinarily well. We have received our winter leather woollen lined jackets and fur gauntlets, and everything is being done to add to our comforts.

I am delighted that you had a visit from Frank Bain. He told me some time ago that he little thought that he would see the site of the Garden of Eden. He was very much struck with the town of Cairo, though when he was in hospital there the heat was intense. He has done his bit faithfully and well.

I had the pleasure of seeing a goodly number of Bulgarian prisoners the other day. This enemy is very fond of sending shells when we are at breakfast, but two can play at that game.

I am longing for a look at the Magazine. Letters and parcels take a long time to reach us from the old country. I greatly appreciate your kindness in sending me such a charming letter. It seems only yesterday since I said goodbye. What a lot has happened from that day to this.

26th

We have received a most excellent parcel of children's garments from the Home Mission Work Party, St Matthew's, Old Meldrum. It is the best parcel we have ever received from those kind friends. In spite of the lady members being involved in patriotic work they have not forgotten about our little ones.

Germany launched an unrestricted submarine campaign, which allowed the current 111 German U- Boats to sink any vessels at will.

30th

Another old boy, Robert Jack, very kindly sends 5s for the Former Inmates' Bed; he expects to be called up shortly.

Miss E. Sturrock kindly doubles her annual subscription and sends us £1, for which we return many thanks.

COALS, COALS

The weather during the past month was cold and sunless. On one occasion the thermometer registered $20°$ of frost. We were obliged to keep the furnaces going at their maximum capacity. Our friends will realise what this means when the price of coke last year was 19s 6d and the present price is 31s 3d.

Who will send a cheque to help? We shall require over £600 to pay our fuel account.

February 1917

The Warden spoke of the dire shortages in food and money for fuel.

"Last autumn when we lifted our potatoes we found we had a very poor crop. We then resolved to take a lesson from the ant, and save a supply for future contingencies. We did this by not eating any! The result is we have enough to plant a large acreage on our farm and garden, and thus we are not under the necessity of buying seed potatoes at the present prohibitive prices."

1st

Today begins the last month of our financial year. We shall require a lot of money in the next 28 days if we are to close the year out of debt.

2ⁿᵈ

One who never forgets us and our needs, Mrs Purvis Russell has sent a most acceptable gift of £5 to help towards our coal bill.

From Private Patrick Hamilton - British Mediterranean Force

I have just received the Christmas number of the Magazine, and I am glad to see that the children spent a happy day. I notice the Roll of Honour grows bigger month by month, but alas! the casualty list is also longer.

Our division did some very hard fighting lately, and were very successful. We received a congratulatory letter from Sir Douglas Haig, in which my battalion was specially mentioned, and we also received letters from other generals including the Australian, so that we feel quite proud of ourselves.

The weather continues to be very severe and it is with great difficulty that we manage to keep our hands from being frost bitten. Kindly remember me to all.

U.S. Administration cut ties with Germany following the announcement of unrestricted submarine warfare. The President spoke of having no alternative consistent with the dignity and the honour of the United States.

An American merchant ship was sunk without warning on the same day as his speech.

8ᵗʰ

Mr James McIntosh, a farmer, who always has a boy from us, has again sent us 10s which we much appreciate.

The Duke of Richmond and Gordon has sent another fine hind.

6ᵗʰ

This is the sixth anniversary of the death of our Founder, Canon Charles Jupp. The time has passed very quickly, and yet, looking back it seems a long while ago. There are barely 150 children here now who ever saw him, and probably not half that number can remember him. But his work continues.

15th

A very valuable gift is £15 from Mrs Haldane, Edinburgh: this includes an additional £5 "towards the extra expenses which have arisen owing to war prices".

19th

James Garden, an old boy who is on his way to join up, has given a most generous parting gift of £2 to the Former Inmates' Bed. He has been a most liberal contributor on several occasions and we are deeply grateful.

From "W" in Edinburgh we have received a very kind contribution of £2 2s. He tells us that he first met Canon Jupp nearly 40 years ago and learned how he used to occupy his time while travelling knitting for the children.

From Private William Robertson - 3rd Seaforth Highlanders - written November 10th

I expect you will be a little surprised when you receive this letter from me, but although my letters are few and far between, I am always thinking of you all in the dear old Home.

There is not much excitement out here but one never knows when something may crop up so we are always well prepared. The weather is much cooler and on Sunday 10th November we had our first drop of rain since April.

I am sure you will be having a lot of dull and dreary weather in Scotland. It will take lots of coals to keep the furnaces going; I know how greedy they are and the great amount of fuel they consume.

The severe fighting in France lately must have added several names to the Orphanage Roll of Honour. It is very sad to think of so many fine fellows being killed in this horrible war.

When you receive this letter it will probably be Christmas. I sincerely hope the children will enjoy Christmas and have the thought of this awful war out of their minds for a few days. I enclose 10s, which will help a little towards extra expenses at the festive season.

20th

This has been a good day as far as money is concerned, and we are grateful indeed to all who have so generously helped to diminish our deficit.

From Mrs Shaw.

I have much pleasure in enclosing £1, and greatly wish I could send more. I often wonder how you exist in the Orphanage when the price of all kinds of food is so high.

Year after year I have tried to pay Aberlour a visit and let my son, Ian, see for himself all I have been telling him. He is nine years old. My brother, Jim, who you no doubt will remember is a piper in the Canadian Cameron Highlanders. He may be in France by this time. I have not heard from him for some weeks, so I am beginning to get anxious, but in these dreadful and sad days one must take things as they come. Please remember me kindly to Miss Tripp and Mr White and any others that I know.

22nd

We are grateful to Mrs Wood for a most acceptable present of 36 rabbits and 4 hares, and to Mrs Guthrie for a roll of wincey and an anonymous gift of tweed from Alloa.

Western Front   German army began to withdraw secretly to the Hindenberg line destroying villages, towns, forests and communications and poisoning water supplies. They completed this secret movement by April 5th.

24th

We are most grateful to the Sunday Scholars of Holy Trinity, Dunfermline for their kind contribution of £2 2s.

Major British attack mounted on the Turks at Kut-el-Amara which fell on February 25th after powerful fighting at what was later known as the Battle of Kut.

28th

Our best thanks for an anonymous gift of £10 from a friend in Edinburgh.

COALS! COALS!

The weather this last month has been exceedingly cold. Snow fell to a depth of 10 inches and one night the thermometer registered 28° of frost. Owing to the kindness of friends we were able to keep our rooms cosy and comfortable.

Mrs Raw's Shirt Guild

This Guild was established in 1902 in Liverpool. Since that date we have received through the medium of the Guild 1293 shirts- a most valuable help indeed.

March 1917

1st

With today we begin another financial year; it will probably be a hard and anxious one, but we can well trust that our daily bread will be provided as hitherto.

7th

Mrs Hepburn and her maid have sent us a very nice parcel of children's garments which are most acceptable.

From Driver David McKenzie - Royal Horse Artillery

Please excuse me from not having written sooner, but owing to recent engagements on this front we have been kept busy. In the first place I hope this finds you all well and making the best of these hard times.

I know it must be very trying for all concerned in the welfare of the old home at present. The sooner this strife is over the better it will be for the country.

I am very tired of it but, of course, we will have to grin and bear it until we have our opponents wiped out.

In the Roll of Honour I have noticed the names of many old companions who have made the supreme sacrifice for King and Country.

I have never had the luck to meet any of the old boys on this front yet.

If all the old boys who come through this strife met at the Old Home I know there would be some rejoicing to celebrate the occasion. Kennie (his brother) still writes to me; he is in France and continues to enjoy good health. He was telling me about an interview he had with Gregor Schuster; they were billeted alongside and it was Gregor who recognised him.

We have fairly got "Johnny Turk" beaten. We are attached to the Anzacs and they are all dash; they will take strong positions at the point of the bayonet, just like the Scotties in France. We occupy the Egyptian town of El Arish after it had been in the hands of the Turks for 2 years.

I hope you had an enjoyable time at Christmas, it passed unknown out here. Trusting this finds you well, with kindest regards to old acquaintances.

P.S. I hope to see the old home once again if I am spared.

Riots, strikes and mass demonstrations broke out in Russia. Demonstrations were against shortages of food and fuel. Police used lethal force to quell the riots.

9th

We have just received a magnificent gift from Mr John Roberts of Wellwood, Selkirk, of a huge bale of splendid cloth for boys' suits. We are sure that the value of this will run into three figures, and it will keep us supplied for a long time. It has come at a time when our stock of clothing was completely exhausted; we had been reduced to making clothes of remnants.

Sgt Albert Morrison, who paid us a flying visit last week, has very kindly sent a generous gift of £1 for the Former Inmates' Bed. It was a great pleasure to see him, but we thought he did not look strong enough yet to return to the Front: we hope he will get an extension of leave.

British troops entered Baghdad having captured it from the Turks. Intense heat of later months halted operations till September.

U.S. president decided to arm all U.S. Merchant ships sailing in areas where German submarines were known to be active. Two British Destroyers and a merchant ship were sunk in the English Channel by German destroyers.

19th

A most acceptable gift in the form of eight bottles of Parrish's Food and four of Cod Liver Oil comes from Mrs Henry Tod, though we hope the worst of the winter is over, this is always a trying time for children's health, and we are grateful for this present.

20th

Mrs Wood has sent us a very welcome gift of 40 rabbits and 2 hares, which will be much enjoyed. We have also received 6s 9d from the children of St Martin's Mission Sunday School in Dundee.

24th

Mrs Mackenzie Murray has this year very thoughtfully and kindly sent a number of packets of seeds of useful vegetables instead of flowers for the children's gardens. These are most acceptable as they had already resolved to make kitchen gardens of their plots.

26th

Many thanks to Dora Jones for the postal order for 2s towards the Former Inmates' Bed.

Middle East - British Invasion of the Gaza Beersheba line with 16,000 troops. Heavy losses sustained in battle against Turks- 4,000 British troops and 2,500 Turks. Troops suffered from acute shortages of water and strong Turkish resistance.

28th

The boys are busy working in the garden now, when the weather permits, digging the ground for our increased vegetable crops.

From Mrs Bradfield (Alice Sedgewick)

You will no doubt be surprised to hear from me. I suppose you will have forgotten about me now, as I know there are so many comings and goings all the time that it would be almost impossible to remember us all. I am glad to say that I have not forgotten you though it is 14 years since I left Aberlour.

I have been in Canada for 10 years now so I suppose I am a Canadian.

A friend of mine in Scotland, who used to be in the Home, sends me a magazine occasionally, so I have been able to keep in touch. I read the Honour Roll and I was surprised to see so many names of the boys I used to go to school with. I was sorry to see that some of them had been killed in action.

My husband went over to England with the Canadians and is with the 3rd Reserve Battalion stationed in Kent.

I have two children aged six and four. I find them great company while their daddy is away.

30th

A valuable bale of shirts and stockings (the latter the work of the Blind Stocking Guild) has come from Miss Varty-Smith of Penrith. This will be an immense help to us.

April 1917

2nd

Ten or twelve inches of snow on the ground this morning and 19° of frost yesterday. We had just given up our furnaces for the summer for want of coke!

3rd

Our good friend, Mrs Sanctuary of Somerset, has sent seven most valuable parcels of clothing for the children. All the garments are just what we wanted and we are very grateful indeed.

6th

Charlie Gibbs has very kindly given us 2s 6d for the Former Inmates' Bed: many thanks.

We are very grateful to the girls of St Leonard's School for a very useful parcel of 30 garments.

Western Front

Battle of Arras opened with the British intending to force the Germans to withdraw troops from the Aisne River.

Three British armies were committed to the exercise, at Arras, at Vimy Ridge and at the Hindenberg Line.

There were heavy losses of British pilots with the superior air power of the Germans.

General Haig decided to continue the offensive into May. At the close of the offensive some weeks later the British casualties killed, wounded or captured numbered 150,000 and the German casualties 100,000.

11th

Mrs Fergus, Nairn, has kindly sent 26 flannel vests from the St Columba's Work Party.

13th

Mr Baily, Brighton, has sent us an interesting collection of pre-Victorian half-crowns in pairs and in good preservation, which will be a nice addition to our Museum.

French advance also took place this month but German air power was superior and the Germans had heavy artillery available and well-defended machine gun positions. French losses amount to 118,000 men.

Mutiny of French troops with some 68 of 112 divisions involved. Soldiers abandoned their trenches and refused to obey orders.

17th

The Rev H Waring sends a welcome sum of £17 10s from St Mary's, Broughty Ferry. They do great things for us at Broughty Ferry!

British troops lost the second Battle of Gaza but take Tamarra on the Tigris River.

20th

We were grieved to hear of the death of another of our old boys, John Banks, from wounds received in the recent severe fighting in France. He was one of our most constant correspondents and invariably wrote in a cheerful strain. We extend our deepest sympathy to his sister and brother.

Only one letter was received from an old boy in April.

From Private George Partridge - 3rd Seaforths

I hope you received my postcard letting you know that I have been wounded. I am glad to say my wound has healed up nicely, and shall consider myself lucky if I always get off as lightly. I was just going into the trenches when I was knocked out. We were sitting down at the rear for a rest, after marching up, and as soon as I had lain down I said to my chum "Oh dear! I could do with an hour's sleep now" I felt very tired and the roads were in a terrible state of mud. One has no idea the condition of Mesopotamia after rain. No sooner had I said I should like to sleep than I got a smack, and you have no idea of how it made me jump. I can assure you it took the sleepiness out of me. I received the bullet through the shoulder, and it came out at the back of the neck. I am glad it touched no bones, or I might have been worse. I was taken down to the nearest dressing station and got my wound attended to. I was kept there until morning and left for the hospital at Amara, where I remained for five days. I slept very well that first night in hospital you may be sure. It was the first time I had slept between sheets for four months. It was a great change from Mother Earth. When the wound healed I was sent further down the river and in a short time I got a nice little job on a ship which was leaving with patients for India. It will be a pleasant trip. I am writing this letter on board the steamer...

...How are you getting on? I often think of the old days and wonder what you are doing. I hope you are all well. I am sure the war must make you anxious at times. I fancy it will soon be all over, as we have fairly got the Turks on the run. It would be a blessing if we could get finished before the summer. I am told the heat is fearful...

...I am pleased to say I received the Magazine, which I always look forward to. It lets me know what is going on, but I do not like to see the casualty list.....I am sorry I am not able to send you any money at present, but I will not forget the Old Home if I am spared to see this through. I am getting very anxious about my brother Ernie. I have not heard from him since I left England. Have you had any word from him? Kindly remember me to all. I wish everyone the best of luck and hope to see you all again.

23rd

We have received intimation from the War Office that one of our old boys, Edward McRae has been severely wounded, and is in a hospital in France. We wish him as speedy a recovery as on the first occasion when he was wounded.

We tender our heartiest thanks to Mr and Mrs Paul for a cheque towards the upkeep of a little boy.

Air War - English Channel Bombers were focused on night time raids and attacks on German airfields to reduce potential strikes from German bombers.

26th

Captain R Lewis A.V.C. sends his subscription for last year and this (£2 2s) adds 10s as a "penalty fine" for having omitted to send last year!

28th

We are grateful to Miss Dudgeon for the price of a shawl she knitted and sold for our benefit.

30th

We tender sincerest thanks to the friend in Tunbridge, who has sent a most valuable contribution of serge and suiting.

COALS, COALS!!

At last we have managed to stop our furnaces, after the coldest and most protracted winter for the past twenty-two years.

Owing to the high price of coals and coke, our account last year amounted to nearly £700, which is the highest on record.

May 1917

1ˢᵗ

We have received an excellent parcel of 51 children's garments from our friends in St James, Inverleith Row, Edinburgh; they are most useful and suitable.

3ʳᵈ

We had a very pleasant visit from Private Donald Coghlan and his brother, Thomas. The former is on the eve of his departure for the front, and we earnestly trust he will be spared to visit us again in health and strength.

From Private William Rattray –

I am sure you will be wondering where I am. I am sorry that I have not written before this but I am far away from home.

We arrived at Durban in South Africa last week. The people are very kind to us, and we are enjoying ourselves. Two months ago we nearly froze to death in Scotland with the frost and snow, but here the heat is overpowering and we can scarcely breathe. We left Bonnie Scotland on February for a far distant land. We had not long to wait for excitement. As we were crossing the English Channel we were attacked by two submarines, which we beat off with the ship's guns. It was a terrible chase, but we were thankful to have escaped.

After that we had to put up with a very rough sea, which caused a great deal of sickness amongst the troops. We had 3 deaths on board ship. We shall be in Mesopotamia in a fortnight's time if all goes well. I hope to meet several old boys there. Kindly remember me to all in the old home and if you are writing to Willie Baker, please tell him where I am bound for.

7ᵗʰ

Once more the annual bales from the Edinburgh Cathedral have arrived, a rare prize they are; they contain no fewer than 1126 articles, all of them most excellent. This number constitutes a record, a truly wonderful event in days such as these, with all the special claims of war on time and money and work. We return our "hottest" thanks to Miss McLaren and her army of indefatigable members.

Air War Western Front

Captain Ball, one of Britain's ace pilots was shot down and killed.

9th

We have received a very nice present of a bath chair in good condition from Mrs Miller of Budleigh Salterton; it will be most useful when we have invalids.

In France, after the spectacular failure of General Nivelle's attack on Chemin des Dames there were French losses of 187,000 recorded and 163,000 German casualties. French troops were demoralised and some frontline soldiers mutinied.

Prime Minister Lloyd George ordered British Navy to start convoy system for protecting merchant shipping. Tactic paid off with fewer British ships lost and German losses rising.

16th

Miss Absolon, Forfar, sends £1 and writes "I feel for you just now with the heavy burden constantly on your mind of how many children are to be clothed and fed in these disastrous times".

Severe fighting in Italy at the Battle of Isonzo with high Italian casualties.

British Warships assisted with the protection of Italian warships off the Albanian coast.

From Private Arthur Mylam - 2nd Seaforths

I have arrived in India at last, after a voyage of 18 weeks, but I wish it had been much longer, for we were lucky in not having one rough day.

We called at Sierra Leone, Cape Town and Durban. At the latter place we stayed three days and gave a concert in the Town Hall, raising £150 for the local Red Cross and YMCA. We were very sorry to go aboard the transport again, where we were packed like herrings in a barrel. We arrived safely at Bombay and were looking forward to seeing the town, but were disappointed as we entrained the same evening for Rawal Pindi, which took us three days to reach. I rather like India, in spite of the heat. It is much better than France, of which I have very unpleasant memories, having been wounded once, and on my return badly gassed. I feel the effects of that poison almost daily. Please send me the magazines from January. I am longing to hear how you are getting on in these terrible times.

Kindest remembrances to all.

[A further letter from Arthur Mylam describing the voyage is included in the July Magazine]

French appointed General Petain to assist in resolving major French troop grievances.

22nd

We have been very grieved to-day to learn we have lost yet another old boy in the war, Fred Dinnie; after serving for some years on farms in the neighbourhood and at Castle Grant, he went to Canada from whence he returned to fight for his country. R.I.P.

Marking a new chapter in strategic bombing, 16 long range German Gotha bombers attacked London from their bases in Belguim. Attack failed because of darkness but about 100 Canadian troops were killed when the bombs landed on a military base.

28th

We are very grateful to Miss Moore for a generous gift of £5 towards the Jumble Sale which is in full swing today.

29th

Our half-yearly Jumble Sale closed today at one o'clock and once again it has exceeded all expectations. A total of £284 was raised beating last May's Sale by £21.

30th

We have had a good number of old boy visitors during these last few days and their contributions towards the Former Inmates' Bed have been on a more generous scale than ever.

No gifts are more valued than those from our former inmates, and the help they render now-a-days is very substantial.

OUR GARDEN

We sincerely thank all those who have kindly favoured us with orders for begonias. We are sold out of all varieties with the exception of the double sweet scented. We can confidently recommend it to all begonia growers.

Double sweet scented- This splendid novelty, which was raised in our garden, should be grown by every lover of begonias. The flower is of rose form; the colour a charming blush; the plants are very free flowering; and the blooms exhale a very pleasing fragrance which is especially noticeable in hot weather. Price is 5s each.

A reference to this variety was made in the Revue Horticole of Paris May 16th 1917.

OUR SALE

A report of the Sale was included in this journal.

"We entered the Sale with anxious hearts and doubtful minds. Fewer parcels had arrived and there was no big windfall from any one donor.

The "fancy" stall was good, "dresses" were fair, "boots and shoes" were very moderate and "men's clothing" very scanty indeed. We did not lack purchasers and they did not seem to lack money. By 1 o'clock on the second day we had made a clean sweep of everything and people went away with money in their pockets, which might have been ours, only we had nothing to sell them!"

June 1917

Note from the Warden

As already announced our AGM is to be held on July 28th.

Increased fares and decreased travelling facilities will probably militate against a large attendance.

Unfortunately we have an outbreak of measles, for the first time in many years. All our patients are going on well so far, but we think it only right to let it be known to any who may be coming to the meeting.

1st

The Countess of Seafield has sent us a garment of her own making for a little girl. We are very grateful and appreciate the kind thought and act.

2nd

We have consented to admit two boys whose elder brother was with us for two years and who left twelve months ago. They are coming by their own desire, being anxious to get away from a very uncomfortable home. The brother refused to return home when his time came to leave and chose to go to farm service instead where he still is.

7th

"Jack's birthday money" is a pathetic gift of 5s towards a summer treat, in memory of a young hero who fell at Gallipoli. *[Pathetic being used in its original form of evoking emotions.]*

British troops launched an attack against German troops holding the high ground of Messines Ridge in Belguim. Germans received sustained artillery attacks as well as exploding a series of huge underground mines under the battered enemy positions. Messines Ridge was captured in a day but with 17,000 British casualties. Germans lost 25,000 troops.

12th

We are very grateful to the Rev Relton Askey and his Sunday scholars of Penicuik for the very kind sum of £1 1s 6d.

The magazine featured a 3 page letter from Private Arthur Mylam who tells of his movements from the time he left Blairgowrie in January and his voyage to Durban and then onto India – it is a fascinating account of the voyage, of time in Durban and then onto India.

We have included much of his letter using his own words – in italics- and made some links between his thoughts and writing

2nd letter June 1917

In this letter I shall try to tell you my movements since leaving Blairgowrie We left on the 18th January at 8 in the morning and arrived at D___ at 3.55 the following morning. ..... We embarked at

once on the "Seang Choon" and at 4pm on the 29th we steamed out on our voyage to the strains of the pipes.

He describes in detail the voyage to Africa in a troop carrier as part of a convoy under escort from destroyers trying to avoid the dreaded German submarines. The journey was long but fortunately not in rough seas. His letter details life on board ship including the celebration of Burns Night and the regular church parades. For a young man from the North East of Scotland, he experiences extraordinary sights and sounds- flying fish and porpoises, massed voices of 1200 soldiers singing hymns. He is an intelligent young man, open to new experiences and he embraces it all.

Saturday 3rd February, we sighted Sierra Leone. As we drew towards the capital we steamed past a magnificent range of hills heavily wooded, quite a treat after days of blue sea. We anchored off Freetown about a mile off shore, to take on coal and water; the coaling being done by niggers, which excited a deal of attention. We were able to get plenty of fruit, paying something like a penny for six oranges and the same for four bananas. I was wondering what your children would think if they could get them for that price.

The ship then moves on after a few days towards Cape Town where the men are able to disembark for a few days.

The whole battalion paraded at 2pm and we were allowed ashore. What an afternoon! You may be sure I made the best of it. I visited the Zoological Gardens, Government House and grounds and the pier, which was magnificent. A sight itself, looking most beautiful at night all lit up (no Zepp scare there). We were all invited to tea by the Burghers which was well spread in a large warehouse. A colossal undertaking it was, for there were over 5000 soldiers in the convoy, but we enjoyed and appreciated it thoroughly. To finish up, I went to the theatre, returning to the ship at 11pm 'dog tired' but happy. Next morning at 7am we steamed out of the harbour, obtaining a beautiful view of that famous sight, Table Mountain, with its usual snowy 'Table Cloth' of cloud hanging upon the top.

The convoy's next port of call was Durban where they were very well received by the 'colonists' as he describes them.

The Ocean Beach Rest Camp was not an imposing sight, it consisted mostly of bell tents and "sand" but it was heaven to us sea-tossed beings. Durban, what a place! Trams at our disposal all hours of the day without cost. Baths and everything free, and a most hearty welcome from the colonists. We had surf bathing every morning. It was great fun diving through the breakers. In the afternoons we went for tram rides, while in the evening it was ten to one if we did not meet some kind colonist who took us to a house of amusement or dinner. Of Durban itself I cannot say too much; it is a most beautiful city, with broad streets and an ideal tramway system, its Town Hall is a magnificent edifice, a sight worth seeing. We had a route march through the city with fixed bayonets, the pipes and kilts roused the greatest enthusiasm. We gave a regimental concert in the Town Hall under the patronage of the Mayor. There was a 'full house', about 3000 people. The proceeds amounted to £160...

...The day we sailed we had a most wonderful send-off, hundreds flocked to the quay. Even their generosity to us when in town seemed not to satisfy them, as they showered on us parting gifts of all kinds. I shall never forget as we left the quay how their voices swelled in that grand old song "Auld Lang Syne". It took me back to the dear old home, when I used to sing it on New Year's Eve in the dining hall. I do not think there was one on that boat who had not a feeling of supreme regret when we saw that most beautiful and bounteous of cities fade away in the distance.

The convoy then makes its way on to its destination in India, disembarking at Bombay before journeying by train to a final destination at Rawalpindi.

Rawal Pindi (sic) is our station. We are all very much impressed with it; my pen cannot describe a tithe of the strange and wonderful pictures which I see every day. The principal streets are long and wide. 'The Mall' is where most of the good shops are to be found...

...Then there is the 'native bazaar' which is full of interest. The shops are quite open at the front. Inside you see natives squatting and pulling away at their curious 'Hubble Bubble' pipes. These natives look as if the last thing in the world which concerned them was the sale of their merchandise. In the cook-shop the cooking is done in the gutter in front of the shop over a charcoal 'Braizier' (sic) the smell of which is not at all inviting to the nose of the European.

It would seem that at the time of writing this letter, Arthur was not involved in any direct fighting so was able to take time to absorb himself in this very different culture where the 'natives' as he describes them were in subservient roles to the troops at all levels. Not being busy fighting created a certain amount of boredom for an active young man and at times he seems frustrated.

After all there is a humorous side to this dull life out here but there is no place like the old country.

Still his thoughts are with Aberlour and the children at the orphanage.

Well Sir! I have done my best to make this letter interesting- you may read it to the children if you think it worthwhile. I guess my composition is poor, as for writing, well: the less said about it the better. ("Mr. White will answer for this")...

...Remember me to all the boys to whom you may be writing.

Air War Britain -Fourteen Gotha bombers attacked London in a daylight raid. Strikes were at the centre of London and 104 people were killed. Public outrage forced British commanders to improve anti-aircraft defences.

16th

Mrs Shaw sends several sums from herself, husband and sons for all of which we are most grateful. She also adds some names to the Roll of Honour including Alexander Steele, who, alas, has been killed.

18th

His Grace the Duke of Newcastle generously sends us £10 10s in response to our appeal for coals. He says "I fear that later on they will be very difficult to get and hope you will succeed in laying in a large supply for the winter".

"Inasmuch" has kindly sent £15 for coals and £15 towards the Lord Kitchener Bed and writes "I am sorry that the bed gets on so slowly. I fear already that the man who saved his country, as there is no doubt he did, as no other man could have got the men he did, is nearly forgotten! However perhaps when the war is over subscriptions may come in more readily".

23rd

Many thanks to a good friend at Carr Bridge for a welcome donation of 10s.

First contingents of American troops landed in France. Troop numbers built to 180,000 by the end of 1917.

26th

We are delighted to hear that Private David Thomson earned the Military Medal on May 16th. He is a stretcher bearer, and won the distinction "for good work during an attack". We heartily congratulate him, and are proud that he is one of us.

Private Ernest Bannerman has sent 4s for the Former Inmates' Bed and Chalmers Thain who has been here today has given 3s towards the same object: we are grateful to both.

New Commander of British troops, General Allenbury was ordered "to capture Jerusalem by Christmas".

OUR SUMMER TRIP

Owing to the high rate of railway fares, and the continuance of this terrible war, we have again decided to abandon all idea of a trip to the seaside. We have been reminded, however, by the receipt of several contributions for this special purpose that our friends would perhaps like the children to have some treat at home.

We shall be glad to receive donations from those who are in favour of our young folks having a day's pleasure in our own grounds.

July 1917

2nd July

The pupils of St Margaret's School in Pitlochry (from Scarborough - possibly evacuated), have sent us a most generous gift of £5 and we return many thanks.

We thank Misses Tweddell for their kind donation towards a summer treat.

3rd

A splendid roll of flannel has been sent by Mrs J.J. Johnstone, for which we are deeply grateful. We are very glad to have it in the summer, for we have to prepare beforehand for the winter.

4th

We are grieved to hear of the death of another old boy, Anderson Auchterlonie, who was shot by a German sniper. R.I.P.

6th

Private Matthew Jack sends a welcome gift of 5s for the Former Inmates' Bed.

Also sends good news of Pte Ernest Partridge, about whom we were getting anxious, as we had had no word from him for some time. We are sorry to learn that Robert Jack is not very well.

9th

An anonymous friend from Edinburgh sends £5 for the children's summer treat. There will certainly be a special treat and we are most thankful for this substantial help.

10th

Sir George MacPherson Grant has sent a most acceptable present of ducks and fowls for our larder.

The British began a major air campaign over Ypres with the intention of sweeping the Germans from the sky before a major offensive at the end of the month.

16th

We are having a very pleasant week-end visit from three old boys whom we had not seen for a number of years: Fred Partridge HMS Patrol had not been for 11 years, and is spending a well earned furlough with us; Pte Alick Masson (ten weeks in the army and expecting to go out with the next draft) and Frank Clisby we had not seen for five years. All are looking well and we hope their visits will be more frequent in the future.

17th

A General commanding on one of the fronts finds time to write us a kind letter in which he says "You must indeed be having a hard time to keep bread in the children's mouths. I want you to feel that I am always ready to come to the rescue as far as I can if you are really stuck for something you badly want. I am not a rich man but my admiration for your Founder will always make me produce something "out of the stocking". Now don't forget that."

18th

We have been very pleased to get a parcel from Nellie Hounsell, a former inmate; her mistress very kindly supplied the material and Nellie made the garments. It is a very useful gift for which we are most grateful.

British forces made a start on the attack in Ypres with 1400 artillery pieces which fired high explosives and gas shells on the German trenches.

19th

Two substantial cheques for coal have lightened our hearts today.

20th

A handsome donation of £25 from J.A.H. has come to cheer us today; £2 for the summer treat and £23 for coals. "I know so well the discomforts created by extreme cold that I can specifically sympathise with other shivering mortals!"

26th

A splendid parcel of shirting, flannel, cloth and dress material has come from Mrs Hamilton Ogilvy; just what we wanted. Many thanks indeed.

The bombardment at Ypres lasted till the end of July when the third Battle of Ypres also known as Passchendale began.

General Haig launched the battle at Passchendale with aim of capturing ground right up to the ports of Ostend and Zeebrugge but strong German counter attacks and terrible mud limited the British to gains of around two miles.

30th

Mr John Macdonald, once a labourer on our farm has very kindly given us £1.

We are very grateful to Miss Donald for 24 pairs of boys' stockings.

In July, as in other years the Magazine contains reports from the AGM and does not include letters from the old boys

A few extracts from the reports to the AGM.

A good number of our staunch friends braved all obstacles and came as usual to encourage us by their presence, and others promised to come to the first meeting after the War is ended, so we shall hope to see them next year.

The boys' gardens presented a fine spectacle of potato blossom; the girls' gardens had a capital show of turnips; all the flower borders were rich with cabbages and kale! Nearly all the work had been done by the boys and it promises to keep us at least from actual starvation during the coming winter.

The formal business included a speech from the Chair:

"A well known clergyman in Scotland remarked some time ago that large areas of the country still knew nothing about the Orphanage, that there is a veritable gold mine still untouched, and that there should be not the least difficulty in raising an extra £1000 a year when it is wanted. It is wanted now, and urgently wanted; every effort must be made without delay to secure new subscriptions."

From the managers' report

There is an increase in maintenance payments thanks to the Government Separation payments and we have to face the fact that these will diminish when the war ends. Permanent endowments (of beds) rose considerably to £3466 for the year.

The average number of children in the Orphanage was 489 or 3 more than the previous year: 95 children left and 113 came.

Our list of old boys who have been killed or wounded in the War continues sadly to grow too long. At present we know of 39 killed or missing. We get very bright letters from lads at the Front, and have had several visits from those who were on leave or had been wounded.

We are proud to know that two, Sgt Albert Morrison and Private David Thomson have won the Military Medal.

From the Diocesan Inspector of Education

General Grade for the whole school - excellent.

From the Medical Superintendent of the Orphanage

Seven children died in the Orphanage in the year to February 1917. Tubercular disease accounted for four deaths, including one of the lungs. The health of the children has been affected by outbreaks of scarlet fever and of measles. Otherwise the health of the children continued to be good.

August 1917

1st

Many thanks to St Peter's, Kirkcaldy, and its Missions for the sum of 14s 1d allocated to us as a donation.

British offensive at Ypres was temporarily suspended due to unseasonal heavy rain turning the battlefield into a sea of thick mud.

4th

Lady Horne, East Haddon, very kindly sent a cheque for £10 10s for which we return many thanks.

8th

Mrs Seely has sent us a nice box of garments from Boston U.S.A. We are very grateful for these, and are fortunate that they have escaped the perils of the seas in these dangerous days.

From Private John McLeod - Australian Forces

I have much pleasure in writing to you as an old boy of the Orphanage back again in the British Isles after an absence of eight years in Australia. I have come over with the Australian Forces as no doubt you expected all your late school boys from overseas would do.

I thought that the climate here might have a bad effect on me after the long absence in such a healthy place as Australia inland.

So far I am all right, but of course I was never strong, especially since I have joined the army. I think it is living in close contact with a body of men, most of whom seem to be suffering from coughs and colds. The Australians are not a healthy lot and the winter was very severe on them.

We had a good trip over, at least as good as could be expected on troop transport. There were 900 aboard and only 3 died. We had 10 days in Cape Town—it has some fine beaches and claims the finest tram ride in the world; no doubt it is the best I have seen; 11 miles around a mountain and along 3 beaches for only one shilling. We were treated magnificently by the towns people.

I have been to London for 4 days' leave. The time was too short to come to Scotland but I expect to get there someday, and I will visit you if possible. I gratified a wish to see good paintings, and accordingly set out to the National Gallery. Most of the paintings I wanted to see were closed up in rooms I could not enter. The English people were very courteous to us, especially the YMCA men who acted as guides for us.

Our camp overlooks the village of A----, which has a fine old church, partly Saxon and partly Norman. The Vicar showed me round one day. The village of F where is situated the smithy celebrated in Longfellow's "Village Blacksmith" is only 2 miles from here.

I have been taking photos but do not think the quality is so good as I am using film not plates.

How is Mr White? I would like to meet him again. I left the Orphanage in 1905, yet it only seems to be a few days. Hoping to hear from you soon.

10th

Flora McQuade has been spending a holiday with us, and has kindly left 4s for the Former Inmates' Bed.

Offensive restarted at Ypres but progress was very slow and limited to a few hundred yards by conditions and stubborn German defence.

16th

Miss Dudgeon has collected the handsome sum of £7 in amounts ranging from 6d to £1 and sends it to us to contribute towards the children's pleasure.

A single British Air Force was proposed and accepted with Air Marshal Sir Hugh Trenchard appointed as its first Commander.

18th

A handsome gift comes today of £25 from Mrs Dunbar, Forres, which considerably helps to relieve our anxieties: she feels more than ever what a great and good work the Orphanage is doing for the children of this country.

Photo from National Library of Scotland's WW1 Collections.

Major battles were fought in Italy where Italian and Austro Hungarian forces suffered major losses of troops. A call was made to the German High Command to stabilise the front with more resources.

From Private Robert Cardno-Gordon Highlanders

Just a line to let you know that I received the magazine you sent all right. I was pleased to get it.

I was very glad to see that the AGM was a success.

I must say I am keeping healthier now than ever before in my life, the open air life (sometimes too open) accounts for that and the feeding, is as good as it can be, Private Bully Beef V.C. (corned beef) being very often the principal diet, especially when in the trenches.

I was very sorry to see the death in action of Anderson Auchterlonie. He was an old Mitchell Wing lad. I hope that Mr White is keeping well, also Mr Kissack. I will finish up wishing you good luck and success in the 43rd year of the existence of the Orphanage.

24th

Private James Speirs from whom we had not heard for some time, kindly sends 5s for the Former Inmates' Bed.

28th

We are deeply grateful to Lord Wimbourne for a splendid gift of venison, which is doubly acceptable at present, when the price of food is so terrible. The children will have a great treat, and the butcher's bill will be lessened considerably. These gifts in kind are of inestimable value to us.

30th

During the past three days we have experienced a disastrous storm of wind and rain, which unfortunately, has damaged our ripening corn. No less than three inches of rain fell.

September 1917

"Wanted: A gymnasium

We are very anxious to provide some good winter evening recreation for the boys in the form of a gymnasium. Our large dining hall will provide the space all we want is the apparatus. We estimate we could make a good start with £25 or £30 and towards this we have received £10.

The value of such a form of healthy recreation needs no enlarging upon. Winter evenings are often difficult to fill up rationally."

1ˢᵗ

We are grateful to Mrs Bell MacDonald and the members of the All Saints' Home Mission for the splendid outfit for one of our boys. They have kindly promised to clothe a girl whose father was killed in the recent severe fighting in France.

We regret to hear of the death of another of our old boys, Alexander Steele, Highland Light Infantry, who was killed in action on April 27ᵗʰ 1917.

He came to the Orphanage 27 years ago, and to him belonged the honour of being one of the boys to have his name specially mentioned in our magazine in connection with a fire which broke out in one of the wings, when he displayed great tact and energy creditable to an adult. We extend our deepest sympathy to his brother.

Major German assault on Russian troops was successful and they took Riga. 9000 Russian Prisoners taken and many others simply deserted their posts.

11ᵗʰ

The Rev Charles Prodgers has kindly sent us the first gift of rabbits this season. They will make an agreeable change in our dietary.

13ᵗʰ

His Excellency Lord Wimbourne, Viceroy of Ireland has sent a further supply of venison. We are very grateful for this valuable gift, which will considerably reduce our terribly high butcher's bills.

From Private William Robertson, 3ʳᵈ Seaforths - Mesopotamia

I am very glad to know that you received the money, but it does take a very long time to reach its destination from here. I was just beginning to wonder what had come over you, and I may say your letter had just taken five months to reach me, so you will see how our mails have been hampered by operations. Now that they have ceased for the summer we are receiving correspondence much more regularly and I am receiving letters almost every day now.

I have seen Baghdad at last, and I do not think very much of it as it is a very dirty town. The population welcomed us in and some of the people tell us some very funny tales of how the Turks treated them. They say that the Turks took all of their silver money and gave them paper notes which were of no value, and many of the poorer class were starving. However, since we have been in Baghdad they have been much happier and have no need to hide their money from us.

We have made big improvements in the town already and in a few years to come one will hardly know Baghdad of old. Most of the hotels are named after our own, such as Hotel Great Britain, and the Imperial Hotel. The Tommies can have a good four course dinner for one rupee and four annas, which is one shilling and eight pence in English money.

I have seen the mosques and the tombs, and there are a few more wonderful buildings but most of the houses are very dirty.

The people dress in all different colours, and their costumes are mostly silk, and they are worth watching as you never saw such beautiful colours in our country.

I had a letter from Mrs Pattison and she said that George Partridge is in a regiment close by. I hope to see him – we will be staunch friends.

The weather is exceedingly hot again, you are like roasted alive through the day and eaten alive at night by the mosquitoes. At present I am in the best of health. I will conclude wishing you all the best of luck and remembering you in my prayers and hoping that the time is not too distant when I may see you again.

14th

A friend sends us a donation to our oatmeal fund. It is most welcome. During the winter and spring oatmeal has been much dearer than flour. The present price is still 51 shillings for 140 lbs; we require 20 x 140 lbs per month to satisfy our young folks' healthy appetites.

15th

Once again it is our painful duty to have to record the death of another of our old boys on the battlefield of France, John Durrant, Cameron Highlanders. He was nine years under our roof, and left to engage in farm work, in which he was very successful. We tender our sincere sympathy to his sister who was also an inmate for many years.

From Private Ernest Partridge - Cameron Highlanders

I am writing to you just before we go to the trenches again to hold the line. I expect to be getting my leave shortly, and when I do get it I shall not forget to come and visit the old Home.

I have been in France now 13 months, and I have mounted the parapet two or three times and I have come back without a scratch. I have been through all the hardships my battalion has been through and they are not a few. I had a very narrow shave on the 9th of April last when a sniper put a bullet through my haversack which was strapped onto my back, and in which were my iron rations and a few other odds and ends. I can tell you, sir, it gave me a fright.

I got my rifle into position as I saw 2 or 3 Germans at the corner of the trench passing along bombs to their comrades who were throwing them at our men lying in the shell holes before the German trench.

My platoon sergeant was lying in the same shell-hole as myself and asked me if I could nail one of the Germans. He said he would take the one on his right. We got our rifles up and he said "Are you ready? Fire!"

When I looked at my target I could see the man's steel helmet fly off his head, he threw up his hands and then disappeared. The sergeant's target was also well struck and I think suffered the same fate. You know all this happened in a few seconds. I will not say more at present as I am not a great writer, but when I come to see you I will be able to tell some short stories of my life in the trenches. I will now draw to a close, hoping you are all in the best of health.

19th

We desire to express our sincerest thanks to the anonymous donor who sent 67 yards of splendid tweed. This gift is of exceptional utility at present, as we had scarcely a scrap in stock. Our boys' clothes wear out in a marvellous manner, especially in the fine weather we have enjoyed this summer, when all have practically lived in the open air.

Western Front Belgium- Focus of British offensive around Ypres switched south. General Plumer decided on a series of small offensives and this tactic was successful at Menin Road and Polygon Wood. Progress was aided by the ground drying out.

Germans used mustard gas for the first time.

25th

We received a letter this morning with great joy. It has come from the Secretary of the Local Government Board on the instructions of the Secretary of State to transmit to the funds of Aberlour the sum of £30 being part of the proceeds of a golf tournament in Sleepy Hollow, New York, a sum received through the Foreign Office. The promoters of the tournament desired that the proceeds should be allocated among institutions devoted to the care of Orphans in Scotland.

The Warden writes that "this has been a great surprise, and forges another link in the chain which binds us in close friendship with our great and powerful ally, and we trust is a foretaste of that strong arm which will help us to secure a glorious victory in the interests of truth and justice".

Middle East- Mesopotamia British and Commonwealth forces advanced along the Euphrates River and defeated the Turks at the Battle of Ramadi.

29th

We were very glad to see one of our soldier lads today- Peter Banks of the Seaforths, who is home on short leave. He has been fighting in France since the beginning of the War.

October 1917

1st

The Warden returned from his annual visit to Braemar, where he had to preach on behalf of the Orphanage and where he enjoyed again, as always, the kind and generous hospitality of Mrs Macdonald of the Fife Arms Hotel.

This year the visit was too late in the summer and the visitors had gone and the church almost empty.

On his return the Warden found a cheque for £350 for the purpose of endowing a bed. This most generous gift is from Mrs Copeland of Stone in Staffordshire. A good many years ago Mr and Mrs Copeland sent 3 boys here, and they have never forgotten the Orphanage. The bed is to be named after the late Mr Copeland- the Richard Pirie Copeland Bed. We are deeply grateful for this handsome gift.

2nd

Our treasurer tells us we will be £600 overdrawn when we have paid the September bills and a few cheques like one for £35 received this morning would help us along splendidly.

3rd

Harry Handforth, an old boy whose ventriloquial entertainments will be remembered by many, has very kindly sent us 10s from "the Front" for the Former Inmates' Bed.

5th

Two valuable parcels have arrived this morning- one containing a large number of most useful garments from our constant friend J.A.H. and the other a roll of flannel from Mrs Sharp of Balmuir.

The weather has undergone a decided change in the last two days, which makes us appreciate these gifts the more; the long, warm, fine days have yielded at last to cold and rain and we have been made to think of winter clothing and fires. The first snow of the season is on our neighbour, Ben Rinnes!

British troops were to continue to drive north to Mosul, a vital oil-producing centre.

Battle at Ypres continued, attacks made on the village of Passchendale without success. General Haig remained determined to capture the high ground outside Ypres.

6th

Yesterday after writing the last entry, we had a heavy fall of snow and the ground was quite white for a short time; there was also frost at night.

8th

The Duke of Richmond has again sent us a fine stag for which we cannot be too thankful.

A few years ago we had a boy here named Robert Sinclair Johnston, and one day he laughingly declared that he would endow a Clan Sinclair bed when he grew up. Alas, he found a soldier's grave when he was only eighteen! Who will undertake the task that can never be his now?

9th

George Tyson, who has been spending a night with us and who expects to be going to the Front soon, has kindly given 2s 6d for the Former Inmates' Bed.

11th

Mrs Henry Tate, London has sent us an interesting and acceptable gift of a large Union Jack; this is to be hoisted on various national anniversaries and duly saluted and honoured.

From Private P.J. Hamilton - British Mediterranean Force

I am back in England again. I have had a warm time of it, and I can assure that I am glad of the rest and change.

Our battalion left S--- in March and we took up our quarters near a ruined city. The statutes were lying broken in the streets and desolation reigned everywhere. We were soon in the trenches, and for eight days and nights we knocked about in mud and water. The weather was simply awful, and we had a lot of rain and snow. During this time I saw some splendid air fights, and our men invariably proved their superiority over the Bosche. The enemy are fast retreating, and our artillery keep them well fed with "iron rations".

After a spell in the trenches we were relieved, but our lot was not much better as we were put into a chalk pit, which, for water, was worse than the trenches. We were then billeted in a prison which was very comfortable. After that we returned to the trenches to make an attack on M. We took three days rations and plenty of bombs. We hardly got into the first trench when Fritz started strafing us with "whizz bangs" and "heavies" one of which struck the parapet in front of me and left me almost stone deaf. I was dug out, and after an hour's rest I felt little the worse except I regretted the loss of my rations.

Just as day was breaking, a terrible din started. It was our artillery barrage, and a minute afterwards we were advancing across No Man's Land to pay back old scores.

We took the first three lines without a halt, and while the guns were being drawn we consolidated our positions. While waiting for the guns to start on our front I got bowled over while watching our men advancing on the right. It is a fine sight to see them moving forward behind a barrage as if they were on a parade ground.

I am in hospital again, but I am getting on all right and hope soon to be discharged.

Please give my kindest regards to all in the Orphanage.

13th

To-day we received the half yearly bales of garments from the Aberlour Orphanage Guild. This gift is always a most generous and welcome gift, one of those gifts we simply could not do without. The total number of garments this year is 603. We tender our warmest gratitude to all who have helped to achieve this remarkable result.

15th

A lady sends 10s from her mother "with many regrets that this is the last donation she will be able to send. She has been concerned with the Orphanage ever since Mr Jupp opened it; he was a great friend of ours. Now he is gone and my mother is waiting her call which cannot be long".

We part from such an old friend with sorrow. May her end be peace and her good works follow her.

16th

The congregation of St Mary's Church Hamilton has sent a handsome contribution of £14 12s.

Convoy of 12 merchant ships escorted by two destroyers were surprised by two German light cruisers. Both destroyers and 75% of the convoy were sunk.

Disastrous Zeppelin raid on Britain led to the end of Zeppelin raids on Britain.

19th

Last night we had a visit from a stoker of the Royal Navy, who thrilled us with stories of his experiences and adventures; and this evening Private Ernest Partridge has come from the front to spend a few days leave; he has much to tell us, no less exciting, and has brought some interesting and gruesome souvenirs of the battle-field which will find a place in our museum. He has also given us £1, which is very generous indeed.

23rd

We are grieved to learn of another old boy, Peter Hogg, having been killed but we have no particulars. R.I.P.

The British again attempted to take the village of Passchendale. The rate of progress was very slow because of mustard gas and dreadful ground conditions. It was not till November 6th that the village fell.

The Third Battle of Ypres was an awful experience for the British with some 310,000 men killed, wounded or taken prisoner to capture a mere five miles of territory. General Haig was criticised for prolonging the offensive despite it becoming apparent that the breakthrough he desired was not achievable.

31st

Douglas Morrison has come today for a short visit at the end of his leave. He is engaged in the perilous task of mine-sweeping; and has had some terrible experiences and narrow escapes; three times the ships he has been on have been blown up. But he seems in high spirits. May he and all others in like states be preserved in their dangerous work. How grateful we ought to be to them!

Mrs Reid has sent a nice rocking horse for our little ones, a delightful gift!

Third battle of Gaza launched with 88,000 troops in seven divisions. They were opposed by the Turks supported by some German artillery. Beersheba was attacked and finally taken following a daring charge by Australian Cavalry at dusk. This secured vital wells which provided essential water to the troops fighting in intense heat. The Turkish Army was forced into headlong retreat leaving the Turkish left flank exposed to further British advances.

COALS, COALS!

The weather during the past month was cold and wet, with occasional snow showers. We managed to struggle along without lighting many extra fires but the time cannot be far distant when we need to light the furnaces. Fuel will then be consumed with a vengeance, one furnace alone requiring nearly a ton of coke a day. Coke is now 31s 3d per ton.

Who will send a cheque for a ton, 10 tons or 100 tons?

November 1917

The weather was exceptionally mild, in fact so much so that we did not have to light the furnaces. We are devoutly thankful for this great blessing as it means a saving of many tons of coke.

1st

All Saints' Day. This is always a bright and happy festival and also a holiday.

The Birnam and Dunkeld Stocking Guild have sent 29 pairs of stockings and socks; we are very glad to have them.

We have received a cheque from a legacy of £300, which is to endow a bed in the Orphanage preferably of the name of Thomson or Wilson. We are rarely without children of these names.

A grand roll of serge has come anonymously from Edinburgh, a valuable present for which we return many thanks.

2nd

We have today received £100 from Lieut.Colonel Sir Philip Chetwode, who is commanding on one of the fronts. It is indeed wonderful that one with such cares and responsibility should be thinking of us and our needs, and give such a tangible proof of his sympathy.

The first three soldiers of the ever-increasing American forces were killed in France.

Discussions took place to consider the establishment of a unified command structure including the defeated Italy. David Lloyd George created the Supreme War Council, including, Britain, France, Italy and the United States.

British Troops drove forward into Turkey trying to establish a wedge between the two parts of the Turkish Army.

7th

Some good friends who for several years have sent a large number of toys for Christmas are quite unable to get them this year and they have very generously sent us a cheque for £10 which is to be expended for the children's enjoyment in whatever form commends itself to the Warden. The children all join in hearty thanks for this very kind gift.

9th

We have had applications today for the admission of no fewer than eleven children!

From Private Robert Cardno - Gordon Highlanders

I was very pleased indeed to get your kind and very welcome letter, and I was glad to see by it that you were keeping well. I was very glad to see by your letter that you were spending a holiday in Lossiemouth. It is not very often that you take a "day off" especially since the war started, and I hope you felt the benefit of it; a breath of bracing sea air usually makes one feel fit.

I am receiving the magazine regularly every month and I read your last one in advance; as long as I was reading the news the thought of "la guerre" never entered my head.

I was sorry to see about another two old boys making the supreme sacrifice. I remember John Durrant well.

I see that Mr Robinson is staying in the Orphanage now. He will be a great help, and no one knows how to treat boys better than he. I hope he is well. Is he organising an operetta this year? They have been such a success in past years, what happy times they were.

We have different concert parties out here, who amuse us when we are out on rest from the trenches, as they have all the latest comics and sentimental songs. The YMCA and the Church Army huts are always open for tired and weary Tommies and Jocks, and it is there we go for the latest news of home.

I have been in a scrap or two since I came out, which I will describe again. I hear the cry "dinner up" so I will close now hoping to hear from you again soon.

Success to the November Sale!

Further losses occurred in Italy where the Germans took 275,000 prisoners and 30,000 soldiers killed or wounded.

British divisions were rushed to try to bolster the battered Italian Units along the River Piave. Mussolini called for Italians to enlist to try to evict the German forces from Italy.

British Troops under General Allenbury had considerable success in Palestine at the Battle of Junction Station which was the source of much needed water for the Army.

Commander of the British Third Army - General Sir Frederick Maule-died of cholera. He was buried just outside Baghdad.

15th

A splendid gift of 71 yards of good tweed has come from Huddersfield; we heartily thank our unknown friend, to whose identity we have no clue.

19th

The Sunday scholars of St John's Greenock, send £2 12s 6d, a useful gift for which we are very thankful.

The Battle of Cambrai in France commenced with the main attack carried out by 476 tanks. Early success was slowed as the tanks succumbed to mechanical failure or were bogged down in ditches.

German troops engaged in battle provided stiff resistance and much of the early British advances were lost.

The US Rainbow Division arrived in France to support the British efforts.

23rd

We have received a letter from Private William Robertson, Mesopotamian Force that it was he who sent 10s acknowledged earlier this month. We are very glad to learn that he is still sound and well.

From Private William Robertson - 3rd Seaforths Mesopotamia

I wonder how you are all keeping in the old Home, I am sure you will have a hard struggle to keep things on a level footing. I have the "People's Friend" sent on to me and I saw a little paragraph concerning Orphanage Funds, and I hope a few more of the former inmates see it and respond to your urgent call. I have not been able to see George Partridge yet as I am a long way from the regiment at the moment.

It is very sad to hear about those little children being killed in London by air raids, and the Germans cannot gain much by killing innocent women and children.

I was very glad to see in the magazine about Albert Morrison's recovery from wounds, and as he was not looking very strong I hope he managed to get an extension of leave. I see that they are still going at it in France, but I am afraid the weather is not very pleasant there just now and wet weather hampers operations.

Now I will conclude, hoping that this may find you all well and sending my love and best wishes to all.

26th

Four little children arrived this evening, three of them for the nursery; our nursery is now quite full, over full, and the head nurse talks of going on strike if we do not stop!

27th

We are grieved to learn that an old boy, Harry Handforth has been reported missing since October 26[th.] There is hope, of course, but hope is slight in such cases.

We are ready for the Sale tomorrow, and wonder what it is going to produce!

29th

The Sale is over; the wonderful result is recorded as £304 12s 4d and if only we had had more stock we could have got £400. There were plenty of buyers who seemed to have their pockets full of money; but by 12 o'clock on the second day we were cleared out. And now for the 1918 Sales; what shall we aim at? Suppose we say £650!

Thirty-two old boys and one old girl were with us during the week.

December 1917

COALS, COALS

We have passed the shortest day and the coldest part of the winter is before us. We were obliged to start our furnaces at the beginning of December, and since then they have been going full steam ahead, and making serious inroads upon the coke we had stored for the summer.

We are deeply grateful to the many kind and generous friends who contribute so liberally to this important fund.

3rd

A friend of the Orphanage has generously given two guineas to the Coal Fund.

Sir Douglas Haig rushed troops to Cambrai to prevent a German breakthrough but decided to withdraw troops back to where they started the battle in November. High casualties incurred for both the British and German troops.

5th

Miss Begbie has, as always, remembered Founder's Day on the 11th and has this year sent a large supply of chocolate bars, enough for everyone in the Orphanage. This is a valuable gift which will be thoroughly appreciated.

The United States government declared war on Austria-Hungary.

7th

The Misses Chisholm of Erchless Castle have sent us their handsome annual subscription of £20, half of which is in support of a bed and half for coals.

The Turks abandoned Jerusalem and General Allenbury entered the City on December 9th.

11th

We have received a good number of contributions today which make us very grateful and tend to lighten our anxieties.

12th

Lady Gordon Cumming has sent us 6 warm and pretty little covers for babies' cots which will be very serviceable.

13th

Mr Sime of Beauly has most kindly given us a large quantity of firewood, ten or a dozen loads. This is a most valuable present which we thoroughly appreciate, and will save our heavy fuel bill as we have many fires that burn wood nicely.

14th

Miss Scott, Consett, kindly sends £1 "to help the old boys' dinner who come *home* a wonderful word "home" to those who have lost it whatever the causes, the sound of it is warmth and welcome".

17th

A most useful gift of 50 yards of flannel has been kindly sent by Mr Roberts of Selkirk.

18th

Our best thanks to the Primus for a welcome donation of £3 3s; to Lord Wimbourne for venison and to Mabel Guthrie for 3s for Christmas.

From an Old Boy (Somewhere in France) Christmastide 1917

Much as I would have liked to be with you in the dear old Home at this season of the year, I have perforce to forego the pleasure, for despite every effort to obtain leave, the "Powers that be" have proved one too many for me.

This to me is a great disappointment indeed, as I have for many years now looked forward to once again eating my Christmas dinner in the old place.

Should I be spared, I hope at no very distant date to visit Aberlour, at least before my return to Africa.

I know that Christmas brings with it a heavy burden in the way of extra expenditure in order that you might provide the usual "good cheer" to the children. This year the burden will be exceptionally heavy, and I would ask you to kindly accept the enclosed small (all too small) contribution to help you.

Old boys and old girls will be thinking deeply about the old home, and conjuring up pleasant memories of many happy days and bright Christmases spent there in long byegone years. I know too that the day will not be allowed to pass without your giving a thought to those of us who can only be present in spirit. And the dear lads who have made the Supreme Sacrifice – they most assuredly will not be forgotten.

Now, allow me this Christmas Day, from the bottom of my heart to wish you all in the dear old Home – from the Warden to the tiniest "wee tot" in the Nursery, the brightest possible Christmas under the present circumstances, and the very happiest of happy New Years – for may it bring peace in its wake.

22nd

We are grateful to Mrs Horder of London for her kind Christmas gift; she sends us a very pleasing report of one of our girls who is in her service.

We also thank Mr T Pilkington, Thurso, for a good gift of venison.

Photo from National Library of Scotland's WW1 Collections.

26th

Mrs Douglas has sent us three splendid boxfuls of garments numbering 290 from the St John's, Forres Work Party. This is a great gift indeed and we return our warmest thanks to Mrs Douglas and all who so generously gave of time, labour, material or money.

28th

We return our best thanks to Sir John Findlay for a valuable present of a sheep, a most acceptable gift.

Don Cossacks revolted against the Bolsheviks and Japanese forces took advantage of Russia's instability and occupied the port of Vladivostock.

Britain, France and US were angry at the move doubting the motives of Japan.

31st

The year closes with a very acceptable gift of two hinds from Mr Grant of Rothiemurchus and an anonymous donation of £1 from Edinburgh.

We fervently thank all our kind friends and supporters for the many blessings they have showered on us during the past year. We wish them all a very happy New Year and trust that peace may reign on this weary earth before the end of 1918.

We have received the following letter from A.H.C. We thank him for compiling the statistics:

"I cannot help thinking the resumé of your Roll of Honour is worth printing again, for it is certainly something to be proud of".

Names in the first list- unwounded and not missing or killed	158
Have been wounded (2 three times, 2 twice and 1 also taken prisoner)	51
Killed in action	36
Missing (one of them wounded)	6
Total	**251**

There is a full account of "Our Christmas" from the Orphanage in this Magazine - *we have included some of the highlights.*

Christmas once again and Peace is not yet on earth! There is bound to be not a little sadness in the festival of Christmas when the peoples of the world are at each others' throats.

Nevertheless, Christmas is Christmas and we did our best to make the season as bright as possible. Those who are fighting our battles abroad are cheery enough; their good heart is indeed one of their most valuable assets in times of danger.

We did rejoice! Many of our old friends, and indeed many new ones, sent us money and contributions. Gifts arrived from all parts, far and near, large and small.

Christmas Eve eventually arrived! Everything had been scrubbed and polished, microscopic dirt had been carried away.

After Evensong most of us retired early. Some of the early birds caught a cinder in their stockings! Christmas morning echoed with the sounds of carols and goodwill. There were 3 celebrations of the Blessed Sacrament. At half past one o'clock dinner was announced, beef, potatoes, plum pudding (carrots instead of plums) and apples. The dinner was certainly a triumph for our cook.

The Warden proposed various toasts. There was a particular note of sadness as he referred to two of our soldier lads, both present, and both "maimed for life in the crash of the cannonade and the desperate strife"; and also one of the two lads had lost three soldier brothers all former inmates here.

The afternoon was spent outdoors, skating and sliding; but the appetite at teatime was not for food but for Christmas crackers.

You can imagine the bombardment of hundreds of crackers pulled almost simultaneously!

At seven o'clock the Grand March and Reel was announced and thus began one of the best Christmas dances ever.

By eleven o'clock the many perspiring faces- everybody knows how vigorously children dance, and with boots on too- were ready but not altogether willing for bed.

January 1918

We wish to remind our readers that Wednesday 13th February, will be the seventh anniversary of our Founder's death. Since that date 649 children have been admitted and there are only 90 children under our roof who were in the Orphanage when he died.

We ask our friends to remember us especially on that day, and pray that continued blessings may rest upon the work he carried on for so many years.

Our Financial year

Our financial year will end on the last day of this month.

In spite of the serious position of the food problem, we have managed to satisfy our young folks' healthy appetites so far.

We were fortunate in securing a splendid crop of potatoes – over 40 tons. We have also had a good supply of meal from the farm but this source of supply is now closed.

1st

The first three letters we opened this year brought us contributions from children. One from St Andrew's, Gartcosh said "Yesterday our children made a present to our Blessed Lord of £1 3s and a halfpenny and a pair of shoes. They wish to send the money and the shoes to help your children."

2nd

We thank Major Coltman for a fine roe deer.

Alas another victim of the War among our old boys, William Bald. We remember him well, though he left young and a good many years ago; he was a merry little fellow.

3rd

When Christmas is past we generally expect a falling off in the number of letters, but this year the stream has hardly diminished at all; as most of them mean money and money is needed, we are not likely to complain.

Miss M.L. Briggs, in long exile in Trinidad because of the war, does not forget us though so far away and sends £2 2s.

The gymnasium is now getting into full swing and the boys say it looks funny to see the roof of the Dining Hall underneath them when they are on the horizontal bars.

4th

Yet another old boy has to be added to our list of those who have fallen in the War; David Pearson had been previously reported as "missing" and now official intimation has been received of his death.

President Woodrow Wilson outlined his 14 point Peace Programme. It was designed to prevent destructive wars and at its heart were the principles of national self-determination and collective security, with disputes to be settled by an international body. The programme though not universally popular with the Allies subsequently became the basis on which Germany agreed to an Armistice in November.

10th

Private Percy Atkin is about to start for Mesopotamia and kindly sends 4s for the Former Inmates' Bed. We thank him for his gift and wish him God-speed and a safe return.

From Private William Robertson - 3rd Seaforths (Mesopotamia)

I received your most welcome and interesting letter dated September 12th. It gave me a surprise, as it is such a long time since I received a letter from Scotland. Of course I knew your writing before I opened the envelope.

I also received my brother Alick's by the same post, and I called it a good day's fishing receiving two letters from Aberlour on the same day.

I was very glad to know that you were spending a holiday at good old Lossie, and I am sure that the fresh sea air will have done you a world of good. I have some idea of the difficulties you will have in making things go round, and I am sure it is no easy matter to feed 500 hungry mouths in these hard times.

I had the pleasure of meeting George Partridge a few nights ago and we had a long talk of the good old times that we used to spend at Aberlour and it was late at night before we parted the staunchest of friends.

We have been on trek recently and I have not been able to send on the £1 as promised, but as soon as an opportunity presents itself of drawing my pay I will do so and send it on to you. It is a pleasure to be able to contribute, and it is much better the money going to the old Home than be spent on rubbish. I have just come back from a short church service, I'm glad to say that I can attend each Sunday. I am the Chaplain's groom, but I help to make things ready for the service. It is a nice easy job I have got, and it is very much better than being with the regiment.

I suppose the children enjoyed their Christmas and New Year. I expect your canine friend, "Luke", will have his old job of chasing the boys to bed at nights!

I expect you hear regularly from the boys in France, it will be very cold there now.

With fondest love and all good wishes

12th

We tender our sincerest thanks to the members of the St Ninian's Work Party, Glasgow for a most excellent contribution of garments for the children.

16th

Another most welcome present is a parcel of 57 good shirts from Mrs Raw's Shirt Guild. This Guild has now sent no less than 1404 shirts and we cannot sufficiently express our gratitude.

20th

Messrs Sinclair and Buchan, Fish Curers in Peterhead, have made us a very acceptable present of a barrel of pickled herrings; it was accompanied by a very sympathetic letter saying they realised we had a large family and we must find it a great struggle to keep things going.

A British force was sent from Baghdad to take over the Russian Oilfields at Baku on the Caspian Sea. The forces reached Baku in August.

28th

Mrs Seely, Boston Mass has sent us another nice box of little garments for children and it fortunately escaped the attention of the U-boats.

February 1918

The weather the whole of last month was exceptionally mild, for which blessing we are devoutly thankful.

1st

We are most grateful for the generous donation received today of £10 10s from Mr Edward Macbean of Helensburgh.

Austro-Hungarian sailors staged a mutiny at Cattara on the Dalmatian Sea.

2nd

Mrs Michael Hill, London, has sent her kind subscription of £2 2s and says "If families of two or three find catering almost impossible it must be terrible with your large family".

9th

The Duke of Richmond and Gordon has very kindly sent us a nice hind, which is more valuable than ever in these days.

12th

Miss Muriel Robinson sends us £1 as a thank-offering for preservation while on a dangerous sea voyage.

13th

This is the seventh anniversary of our Founder's death, which we do not forget in our Ash Wednesday services.

From Gunner David McKenzie - Royal Horse Artillery

I now have a favourable opportunity to write a few lines after a long silence. Of late I have not had much time to write; in fact I have gone for a whole week without a wash. Owing to our quick movements of Horse Artillery we do not get much time to dream. I trust in the first place that this finds you well and happy, as I am in good health.

Since our big push commenced in Palestine we have had a pretty rough time. I am sure you have read with pleasure all our recent successes.

On the last day of October we started off on the march as a battery of the Royal Horse Artillery attached to a brigade of Australian Light Horse. We were doing about 30 miles a day and resting two days for the first week or so.

We got to a point 30 miles south of the famous biblical town of Beersheba. At this point all was ready for the word "go" and then operations began. Our brigade remained there a few days after the town fell, and then we had a few more marches to another part of the line. Since then we have visited Jaffa or Joppa, and we were even among the first troops to enter the seaport.

I will not say more about the fighting as the Censor might not care to have too much said about operations.

To tell you the truth I have eaten oranges until I was sick, and even then ate them till I was back in my usual condition. One has not the slightest idea of to what extent they are grown out here. I regret I could not send you a few hampers.

Photo from National Library of Scotland's WW1 Collections.

Jaffa was evacuated several months ago. It is a lovely place, situated on the slope of a hill; the sea washes on the walls of some of the houses.

I am only sorry that I have not had the pleasure of paying a visit to the sacred town of Jerusalem. I have spoken to several Jewish people and they have told me all about how the Turks treated them. Their stories are terrible, and they all make us welcome visitors I can assure you.

Kennie is still doing well in France, he writes to me occasionally. I do not know where my other two brothers are at present.

Time is getting along. We are in 1918 and still the strife goes on.

With kind remembrances to all old faces I know.

P.S. Let us all hope that we shall spend our next Christmas together in the big dining hall, then there will be some rejoicings.

Renewed fighting on the Eastern Front involved German forces and the Bolsheviks. Troops were sent into the Ukraine and towards Petrograd, the Russian Capital.

18th

Miss J.D. Forman has forwarded us the very gratifying sum of £7 4s 6d, which has been collected in boxes in shops and hotels in Edinburgh. Miss Forman has carried out this work for many years, and we are very grateful for the labour she has expended on it and for the profitable results. We are pleased to send her six more boxes.

Two fine parcels containing 80 garments have arrived from Holdenby Rectory, the work of Miss M Barrett and other friends. We beg them to accept our grateful thanks for this valuable addition to our stock of clothes.

20th

Mrs Copeland who recently endowed a bed in the Orphanage is now very kindly going to give £10 a year towards the support of a second child in whom she is interested.

25th

We have very gratefully received 2s 6d from William Garden, 3s from Kate Robertson and 7s from Sarah Graham, all for the Former Inmates' Bed.

Following the collapse of the Russian Army in the light of the Russian Revolution, Turkish forces re-occupied some of the facilities at Baku on the Caspian Sea.

27th

One of our staunchest friends, a great sufferer, never loses his interest in "our" Orphanage and has again sent his annual subscription of £2 for maintenance, 5s for the St George Bed and 5s for the magazine; we are truly grateful and our prayers and sympathy are for him in his pain and weakness.

Bolshevik revolutionaries were forced to sign a stern peace treaty with Germany. Rebels had to give up control of Ukraine, Finland and the Baltic States.

German troops continued to occupy Ukraine as its grain was vital to prevent the wholesale starvation in Germany.

OUR GARDEN

For some years we have been rather proud of our sweet peas. Owing to economic conditions we have had to replace them with potatoes and cabbages.

Through the kindness of a friend in England who is a noted horticulturist, we have been favoured with a small specially selected stock of what he describes as the sweetest sweet pea in the world. Its name is Mother of Pearl. As long as stocks last we shall be pleased to sell packets of this novelty containing 13 seeds for 1s post free.

(Is this a sign that Aberlour was ahead of its time in 1918 with Mail Order of plants, seeds and bulbs?)

March 1918

EASTER

Our gardens had a fairly bright display of daffodils and other spring flowers, giving their eloquent though silent message of resurrection life.

Amid the carnage on the western front, Easter truth and Easter hymns were doubly welcome, and could not fail to lift in some measure the overhanging pall of gloom.

1st

We embark this month on the forty-third year of our existence, the days are very cloudy and anxious but past experience, and not least that of last year, forbids us to be despondent.

We are very pleased to get a letter from William Thomson with a generous enclosure of £10 for the Former Inmates' Bed and the magazine and to know that he is doing well in his trade.

4th

We return our best thanks once more to the congregation of Christ Church, Morningside , for their valued contribution of £10 to support a bed for another year.

6th

We are most grateful to Mrs Evans-Gordon for £10 10s, which she has again collected for the support of the Stirlingshire Bed for another year.

11th

We are most grateful to "Interest" for a generous cheque for £10, part of which is for begonia and sweet pea seeds and the greater part a donation to the general fund.

13th

George Paines sends us a very generous donation of £1 half for the Former Inmates' Bed and half for the magazine. We wish him every blessing on his approaching marriage.

From Private George Partridge - 3rd Seaforths

I now take the greatest pleasure in writing you a few lines in haste to let you know how I am always getting on.

I am now in Egypt, as you will see from my address, and so far I like the country. I do not know how long the battalion will be here, probably till March. However we will not go back to where we came from. I am not sorry we have left that part of the globe, for really I was what you could call fed up. This country is pretty much the same, but not so desolate and more civilised. We have everything we could wish for here, such as YMCA and canteen and a picture house where we can spend nights so we count ourselves lucky.

We had a fine journey out, it was very hot while we were crossing the line and we were going about in our bare feet and shirt sleeves. I don't suppose you could do that in England at present! There were a few nights when we were going about in the dark and had to stop smoking. There is nothing like being on the safe side. It would have been a nice catch for the Hun if he had spied us. We managed to land safely without his submarines getting us.

I received the magazine the other day and will hand it over to W. Robertson the first time I see him.

My brothers Ernie and Fred are, I am pleased, to say quite well.

Well I hope to be on seven days leave soon but not to "Blighty", worse luck. I am longing to see old faces again. I am sorry to say I had to leave Arthur Mylam behind in Mesopotamia, but we had two or three days together before I left, and had many a talk of bygone days.

I will now close as I am feeling very tired. Goodnight and remember me to all.

14th

Private Edward McKay has been paying us a short visit while on leave from the Front and he left again this morning. He is looking splendidly well, and it has been a great pleasure to see him.

20th

A lover of children sends a most welcome gift of £5 for which we return many thanks.

Western Front France

Germany planned a knock-out blow on the Western Front aware of the imminent arrival of very high numbers of US troops. Troops transferred from Russia following the Peace Treaty so considerable moves of divisions and Germany had numerical superiority over the British and French.

21st

A most delightful parcel of black and white check scarves for the boys from the Women's Emergency Corps in Edinburgh; these are most acceptable and will be much appreciated.

German forces started the conflict, named Operation Michael, with bombarding the British troops for 5 hours with artillery, gas and explosive shells. Germans, aided by thick fog, overwhelmed the thinly spread British.

Fifth Army collapsed in confusion but Byng's Third Army was more successful in stopping the German advance and withdrew across the Somme leaving the Germans with less gains.

Two days later the Germans began intermittent bombardment of Paris leaving 256 Parisians dead and 620 wounded.

28th

We today received several parcels from Mrs Sanctuary containing 151 garments; a most acceptable present for which we are grateful indeed.

Miss Dixon has sent a delightful gift of 24 blankets, for which we cannot be too thankful.

Germany broke through the juncture of the British Third and Fifth Army. They were aiming to make for the ports of Northern France.

General Haig rushed troops to plug the gap but the French sent only a few troops to assist.

Marshal Ferdinand Foch was appointed as Coordinator of all British, French and American forces in the Western Front. Foch was concerned to stop the German offensive creating further damage to the British line and more French troops were rushed in to assist. The Third Army under General Byng stopped the German advance with support from the air.

31st

The Countess of Seafield and Mrs W. Stewart came to see us today, and we had much pleasure in showing them round the Orphanage, and in particular the Clan Grant Bed, for which the Countess collects and supports annually.

German troops began to concentrate on the areas south of the Somme.

German forces took Montdidier and were within striking distance of taking Amiens. Fresh British and French troops stopped the advance some 10 miles east of Amiens.

April 1918

1st

A most encouraging opening to the month is a valuable cheque for £20 from Sir Peter and Lady Lumsdaine, who never forget us and our needs.

The British Royal Air Force was created.

2nd

We are grateful to the Sunday scholars from St Magadelene's, Dundee for the very useful sum of £2 0s 2d.

3rd

20 St Mungos' Sunday scholars at Balerno collected 2s 6d on Easter afternoon and sent it to us.

4th

A very touching gift is "Wee Jimmy's Treasury Note for the St George Bed"; wee Jimmy was called to his rest in January. We thank his parents for sending us this note, and deeply sympathise with them in their sorrow.

General Ludendorff called a halt to the German offensive Operation Michael as he recognised there was no hope of victory along the Somme. The British and French had suffered 240,000 casualties with German losses equally severe.

9th

Some most valuable gifts have been received with great gratitude from Mrs. Scott of Tunbridge Wells; they are a parcel of very useful articles for the Sale which will fetch good money, some beautiful warm blankets, and a roll of serge. This is grand!

General Ludendorff switched his offensive to a narrow front on the way to the Northern Channel ports.

The Germans achieved a break in the British line about 30 miles wide.

General Haig issued orders prohibiting further retreat.

"With our backs to the wall and believing in the justice of our cause, each one must fight on to the end".

13th

Mrs Mackenzie Murray has again sent the children a number of packets of vegetable seeds for their gardens, which are thus made doubly profitable. Very many thanks.

Some days later the British and French halted the German drive along the Lys river, helping to ensure the failure of the German forces to reach the ports of Northern France.

17th

Miss Pilkington's maids, Bournemouth, have sent a most excellent parcel of children's garments made during Lent, and we are very grateful to her and to them.

From Private William Robertson - 3rd Seaforths

Many thanks for your ever welcome letter and also for the Magazine, which is the first copy I have received for months.

The magazine brought very cheering news with it, and I was very pleased to see that the November Sale was such a great success.

My word you must have had a busy day and I can just picture the boys putting their Sunday Clothes up for auction! So many changes have happened lately, and it was only a few days ago that I could draw some money. To tell you the truth I have not been right settled since the end of last year, but now I think that we have reached our destination, and we are making ourselves as comfortable as possible in our new surroundings. This is really a lovely climate and it is a great change from Mesopotamia. We have one consolation, and that is that our mails do not take nearly so long to reach us from home.

I saw George Partridge on Sunday and we had a nice quiet chat after the evening service.

I am sorry that I cannot give you a description of this country and of the wonderful sights I have seen but perhaps later I may be able to write and tell you about it.

I send my love and best wishes and I am looking forward to the time when I may be able to see you all again.

20th

Our constant friends at St. James, Leith have again sent £10 from the Sunday Schools and Bible Class, which supports a bed for a year, and we return our most grateful thanks.

Baron Manfred von Richenstein, German ace fighter, was shot down and killed. He was buried with full military honours by the British.

23rd

Miss Amy Varty Smith has forwarded a fine parcel of stockings, the work of the Blind Stocking Guild, for which we cannot be too thankful.

Surprise amphibian assault by the British curtailed attacks by German submarines operating from Ostend and Zeebrugge.

British vessels attacked Zeebrugge harbour unsuccessfully as German raiders were still able to leave the port. Similarly attack on Ostend was unsuccessful.

29th

Very many thanks to Maggie Milne and Private Percy Hay for 5s and 10s respectively for the Former Inmates' Bed.

30th

We were delighted to receive a letter and cheque for £10 from the Rector of Christ Church, Trinity. "The £10 has been raised by boxes by adults and children in our congregation by Lent Savings. I thought the result last year was good but we have doubled it this year. If the War has done nothing else it has taught the joy of giving". We are very grateful to all these kind friends.

May 1918

1st

Before leaving Stromness for Aberdeen, the Rev D. Gasking sends us 11s being Lenten Offerings from St Mary's, Stromness. We are very grateful to our friends in Stromness and wish Mr Gasking every blessing in his new work.

Romania surrendered after signing the Peace Treaty of Bucharest. They had suffered the loss of 400,000 troops in the conflicts.

6th

Private James McLellan has been spending the weekend with us, and has kindly given us 5s towards the Former Inmates' Bed.

Another magnificent gift of garments has come from Miss McLaren and the members of the St Mary's Cathedral, Edinburgh, Work Party; it contains 1139 articles, 13 more than last year which in itself was a record. The garments are of all sorts and sizes, something to suit everybody; indeed, it means two garments for each child in the Orphanage. We are particularly struck by the number of shirts, 200, we depend much on this Guild for shirts now and cannot have too many, as we always have 600 in use at one time.

11th

Mr Curtis has kindly sent his annual subscription of £1, for which we are very thankful. He tells us that he puts back numbers of Aberlour Magazines into parcels of books for the troops, on the chance of their falling into the hands of any to whom they may be of interest. This is an excellent idea; some old boy with whom we are not in communication might get hold of one.

We have received a most valuable present of 600 earthenware mugs from Messrs Cartwright, Edwards, Langton, through Mr Hall of that firm.

We always try to be very careful with crockery, but, somehow, it will get broken at times and it is very expensive to replace.

17th

The Princess Royal has again sent her valued annual subscription of £5 towards our funds for which we are very grateful.

From Private Harry Lay - Regiment not recorded

I received your most welcome letter, for which I must thank you very much. I am going on a bit better now and I hope this finds you in the best of health. I was wounded in the side, and there are one or two of my ribs broken and some of them are bruised. I still have a large gash in my side, but think it will heal up now after the operation. We are having lovely weather in England, how is it in Scotland?

The food we got in Germany was very poor stuff, and very little of it. We got one ration of bread at ten in the morning, about one inch thick. At one o'clock we had some dirty water supposed to be soup and the same at six- no more bread. But when we got our parcels from England we never looked for anything; what we got we used to give to the Russians, for they never got any parcels. The Russians died in dozens every day there, and it used to take the wind out of me, for I was very nearly gone once myself but thank God I came through it all right and I often think of how good He has been to me. I was only eight months a prisoner in Germany, but it was long enough for me in the state I was in. We all got our parcels quite regularly. I trust this finds you in the best of health.

20th

We have gratefully received a thank offering of £2 from one who has just heard that a loved one who had been missing for nine weeks is alive though a prisoner. We rejoice with the donor in her joy.

24th

A base-ball match has been played on our field this afternoon between two teams of Canadian woodcutters who are at work in our neighbourhood. In our hilly country there are not many suitable fields to be found so we are lending them ours. A number of visitors, both officers and men, asked to be shown through the Orphanage and were evidently much interested in everything.

26th

Our girls are all resplendent today, Trinity Sunday, in new straw hats, the kind and generous gift of Mrs Clutterbuck. They not only look cool and fresh but are very pretty and dainty, and all the wearers are very proud of themselves.

It has but one drawback, that it makes the boys look rather rueful at their own somewhat badly worn Glengarrys! These caps have lasted the most extraordinary time - we wonder how many of our readers have made their hats last for ten or twelve years!

Third German offensive was mounted by General Ludendorff on the Western Front.

He aimed to prevent the French from sending reinforcements to the British in the north of France where the Germans planned an offensive. Major bombardment by the Germans with 4600 artillery shells and seven divisions of troops led to the capture of Chemin des Dames and an advance on the Aisne river.

29th

Another Sale is over and has again beaten all records.

30th

Mrs Clutterbuck has sent us a good quantity of glucose, which we shall be very glad of.

Early success convinced the Germans to press forward towards Paris. French with reinforcements from the US Expeditionary Forces prepared for action on the Marne River.

Fighting was fierce but the combined troops managed to halt the German advance and captured the village of Cantigny.

June 1918

1st

The month has opened auspiciously with brilliantly fine weather, which the children are greatly enjoying; they live almost entirely in the open air, and the long light days pass all too quickly with bathing in our large swimming pond, cricket and other summer games.

US troops went into action against the German troops threatening towns on the Marne River. With help of French support, the US division forced the Germans back across the Marne.

4th

We were delighted to receive a cheque for £41 from Miss Fowler Jones on behalf of the Yorkshire Bed. We heartily congratulate her and thank her for the great success in collecting this sum.

Fourth German offensive was carried out but deserters had warned the US and French troops of the plans and thus proposed link up of two German forces failed. Heavy losses on both sides and little territory was gained.

7th

Mrs W.M. Forsyth, Aberlour has kindly given us a ton of firewood. This is a very acceptable gift, especially at this present time, when we have great difficulty in obtaining coals.

8th

One good and kind friend, Miss K Macdonald writes: "The porter at one of the hospitals I visit was showing some pieces of a German aeroplane which had been brought down not far off during the last raid. It occurred that if the boys have no such trophies in their Museum, they might like it, so I asked him if he could spare a bit, and he gave me the piece of pipe which carries the petrol from the oil tanks to the engines". We are very glad to have this souvenir.

12th

One of our old boys, Private James Macdonald, paid us a visit today. He has recently been in hospital and had his right arm amputated owing to the effects of serious wounds. He was very bright and cheery in spite of his disability.

14th

Lieut. General Sir Philip Chetwode, Bart has kindly sent £20 in support of two beds.

From Private Robert Cardno - Gordon Highlanders

It is quite a long time since I wrote you, but I have been keeping well, despite everything. Things have been exciting this while back out here, and our battalion has been in the thick of it a few times, and have also been mentioned for good work done. At one point of the line where Fritz was advancing a German transport column came right through our lines but did not get far. The whole thing was captured including a field kitchen, containing soup (I never tasted it but those who did, said it was good) and there was also a good supply of British bully beef among their luggage which they never got the chance to enjoy. Another time All Highest's famous Prussian Guards made an attempt to drive us out of our positions but with the Scots giving them rapid fire they never got half way across "No Man's Land", so they nipped back to their own positions and lay quiet all day.

It was pathetic to see the peasants leaving their homes as the Huns were drawing nearer, feeble old men and women with their children carrying as much of their valuables as they could, some waiting till the last moment in case Fritz did not get as far, which often brought them under heavy fire.

I am very thankful to have come through the last battle safely.

A friend of the Orphanage writes nearly every week and sends comforts. I write a letter to her whenever I have the chance, but under the circumstances a field postcard has to do, especially if we are in the trenches.

I hope your May Sale will be a success, as all your funds will be needed with the price of every commodity being so high.

I must close now hoping this finds everybody in the home in the best of health and spirits and living up to the old motto of "keep smiling".

In Italy the Battle of the Piave River took place with the Austro-Hungarian forces fighting against the Italian troops. Attacks were not successful and British and French participated in a fierce counter-attack which stopped the Austro-Hungarian army from making significant gains.

18th

The Misses Tweddell never fail to remember our children's "Summer Outing" Fund. They have sent 10s 6d towards that object.

19th

We are glad to know that another of our old boys, Private Robert Lockhart, has been awarded the Military Medal.

21st

We are grateful to Mr Calder, Cawdor, for a donation. He writes to say that the boy we sent him is doing well and always does as he is told.

US 2nd Division launched an attack against four German Divisions and despite being outnumbered they launched a succession of attacks over a period of three weeks and had success in clearing the German forces from the desired areas. US have had 1800 men killed and 8000 wounded in this offensive.

US General Graves had orders not to get involved in Russian politics but their role was to prevent the Japanese who have garrisoned Vladivostok from taking over the port permanently.

24th

We deeply regret to learn that an old boy, Patrick Hamilton, already three times wounded, is now reported missing. He took part in the terrible landing at Sulva Bay in Gallipoli.

Joint Anglo-French force occupied the port of Murmansk and later Archangel and Vladivostok.

25th

Mr Heron Wilson noted in the last month's magazine that the girls had received a present of new straw hats, which had put the boys' caps rather into the shade. "As a staunch believer in the equality of the sexes" he has sent a handsome cheque for £25 "to right this freak of fortune". We send him our best thanks, and are losing no time in ordering the caps.

29th

The children began their summer school holidays yesterday in great glee; the weather turned brighter and warmer at once, and we hope it will continue so!

July 1918

1st

We return very best thanks to the Sunday Scholars of St John's Coatbridge, for their most welcome contribution of £3 3s 9d.

A most excellent and valuable parcel of garments has been sent by Miss Clark of Avenel from the Melrose Branch of the Home Missions Association and we return best thanks.

5th

Many thanks to the donor of £5 towards a summer treat for the children also to Edith Keith for 3s 6d for the Former Inmates' Bed.

10th

An old boy, James Higgins, whom we are very pleased to see after 14 years, is spending a short holiday with us, and has kindly given £1 to the Former Inmates' Bed.

13th

Another old boy, Robert Henderson has come on a little visit and generously gives £1 to the Former Inmates' Bed.

The murder of several of the Russian Royal Family in Siberia by the Bolsheviks was reported.

15th

Lady Sempil has sent us a tartan bedcover for the Clan Forbes Bed, it looks very nice. Our row of tartan bed covers is growing.

Western Front France

German forces opened their 5th offensive of 1918. Germans were planning a diversionary attack along the River Marne to draw opponents' troops away from northern France.

German Commander hoped to cut through the British lines and seize the ports along the English Channel. French subverted the plan and French, British and US forces prevented the Germans from exploiting their bridgeheads on the Marne River.

18th

The Cupar and District Association for the Co-ordination of Voluntary Work Associations, has most generously sent us through their Hon. Treasurer, Mr R Pagan Osborne a valuable contribution of £15, being a proportion of the proceeds of a fête recently held at Tarvit.

The Germans lost 500,000 troops in the various offensives while US troops were arriving at the rate of 300,000 a month. Short of troops General Ludendorff planned a measured withdrawal.

19th

Seven little "Blue Cross" workers have offered to keep a little girl aged about nine years; we have gladly given them the name of one who has no parents living, and shall be very grateful indeed for their kind help and interest.

Second battle of the Marne took place, Germans suffered serious collapse and German General called off proposed attacks on the British in Northern France.

Britain's top fighter pilot, Edward Mannock was shot down and killed by German ground fire.

23rd

Our generous friend J.A.H. has sent us a handsome gift of £20 towards our coal bill. With coal at its present price this will help us towards a store for the winter.

25th

The day of the Annual Meeting -reports below.

Our May Sale was such a phenomenal success that we are anxious to have another record one in November. We can sell everything that is of use. New and left-off clothing, especially ladies' dresses, men's suits, boots and shoes, curtains, furniture covers, fancy articles, books and popular magazines are in great demand.

When the Magazine carried a feature about some aspect of the Orphanage life there were no printed letters from the Old Boys.

Report of the AGM - 25th July 1918

The Annual Report of the Managers was submitted and Mr McCorquodale's comments were reported in the Elgin Courier.

I think that the managers can congratulate themselves and those who lived and worked for the Orphanage that the public had been so good to them to give them the money necessary to carry on the work. The managers emphasised in their report that the cost of feeding the children was double what it was a few years ago but there was no doubt that everything was quite satisfactory.

An increase of £350 in voluntary contributions was noted. Such results did not come by accident but by the excellent way in which their establishment was managed.

The work of Canon Jenks, Rev Mr Kissack and Mr White were particularly noted.

Canon Jenks praised the efforts of the Bishops across the UK for the way they had acted to respond to the serious financial problems the Orphanage faced the previous year.

The visitors looked over the gardens, which are now almost entirely devoted to the growing of vegetables. Mr White of late has been specialising in the growing of tomatoes, and he bids fair even to beat his fame as a grower of begonias. It is quite within the mark to say that the majority of the plants carry anything from 20 to 25 lbs of fruit!

The Manager further reported:

The Orphanage is a home, and events of home life run quietly and smoothly; they are full of interest to those who are in the midst of them and take part of them, but home life would not be home life if its trivial rounds were chronicled.

We rejoice to say that neither in health nor in necessaries of life have the children hitherto suffered from the war. The children are as strong and healthy as ever.

We know of more than fifty of our old boys who have fallen in fighting for their country, and the list is undoubtedly much longer, three have received the Military Medal and one the Distinguished Conduct Medal, we continue to receive many letters from those now at the front.

Our boys rendered valuable service in the garden and on our farm, and very materially assisted in the production of food, in saving wages and in reducing the cost of maintenance. We were able to sell several tons of potatoes in the Spring.

August 1918

1st

Inspector Allan, Dundee, who paid a visit today to see some children in whom he is interested, very kindly gave a donation of £1 for our funds, for which we are very grateful.

5th

Many thanks to the Sheepwash Scholars for 6s 6d collected since the end of June. We appreciate their kind help.

As part of the continuing Battle of the Marne, the Germans were forced to retreat and the second Battle of the Marne ended on the 6th of August. Germans had faced catastrophic losses and those surviving are suffering from increasingly poor morale.

7th

The Rev Charles Grubb sends a welcome sum of £2 8s for the Lord Kitchener Bed; as the endowment of this bed is already completed we have proposed the sum should go towards providing a Union Jack cover and a brass plate for the bed.

Photo from National Library of Scotland's WW1 Collections.

From Private Percy Hay - somewhere in France.

I now take the pleasure in writing you a letter. We are having beautiful weather out here which means a lot to us, but the heat inside the tanks is awful. I have been out here a short time now, but

I have not come across any of the old boys. I do hope to meet in with some of them so as to have a chat about the days we had at the Home. It is on the battlefield that all our childhood days come back to us, and the happy days we had at the old home. I am glad to say that I am keeping well. I have seen some terrible sights, and the Germans destroy everything they can see. I passed a cemetery the other day and the crosses were broken and scattered everywhere. The churches seem to be one of their chief places of destruction, but a time will come when they will pay dearly for their wickedness.

They are getting an awful smashing up just now as you will see by the papers. I am glad to say I have had my baptism of fire as I was always longing to get at the enemy. I wish I could tell you more, but I am sorry I cannot until this great battle is over; but you will see from the papers how we are progressing, and I hope it will bring the war to an end, and I pray for the day we shall all be together again. I hope to be with you at Christmas or New Year. I will have to conclude, wishing you all the best of wishes at the Home—

Your sincere friend, Percy

General Sir Douglas Haig spearheaded the Amiens Offensive which eventually led to the clearing of the rail road to Paris and the defeat of the German offensive with heavy losses.

12th

Lady Caroline Gordon Lennox has sent us a delightful parcel of woollen garments, all her own make, for our little ones, which we very much appreciate.

16th

J. A.H. who so often figures as one of our most generous friends, has sent us £30 to buy cloth for boys' suits; we were very badly in need of this for we had not a yard left, and many clothes wanted renewing.

20th

We thank Mrs Moyle Rogers for 6s and the Sunday Scholars of Holy Trinity, Keith for 8s 6d.

Second Phase of the Amiens Offensive started and with combined French, British and US forces the German forces were pulled back in what amounted to a general retreat.

24th

Kind thanks to the Duke of Richmond and Gordon for a fine haunch of venison; to Sir George Macpherson Grant and Sir John Findlay for grouse; and to Mr J C Harvey, Dinnet, for 40 rabbits.

28th

We received a valuable addition to our Museum and to the decoration of our halls and rooms in the form of a large collection of curios, stags' heads, pictures etc.

These were the property of our good friend "Inasmuch" who had expressed the wish that they should be sent to the Orphanage. We shall treasure them much both for their own sake and that of their late owner; and we are very grateful to Miss Butterworth, who has taken so much trouble in having them packed and sent.

First Army of American Expeditionary Force opened attack on St Mihiel.

CONCERT AT CULLEN

On August 9th the Dowager Lady Seafield gave a concert in the Town Hall at Cullen for the purpose of raising some money towards the endowment of the Clan Grant Bed at the Orphanage.

The Hall was very full and the programme was a most excellent one, and the various items were thoroughly enjoyed by the audience who demanded many encores.

The Young Countess of Seafield played a cello solo which was most warmly applauded as it deserved to be.

A local troupe of pierrettes provided several delightful items and at the end of the concert the Warden ventured to express the hope that they would come over to Aberlour at no distant date and entertain our children.

The concert realised over £28, and we desire to tender our sincerest thanks for this substantial help.

Photo from Aberlour Child Care Trust Archives.

Collecting sphagnum moss

The Journal also records the trip that fifteen of the senior boys made to Tulchan Lodge, Advie (a neighbouring village) to collect sphagnum moss which was widely used as an antiseptic for dressing wounds. They went with the Warden and with Luke, his faithful dog.

The notes record that there were weeks of anticipation and excitement about the trip which was for a week.

"We had to take with us almost everything that we should require, except bedding. When we reached Advie we found two carts waiting for our luggage. We soon tumbled the luggage in and loaded up with some bread and biscuits at Mrs Allan's shop, the only shop Advie possesses. Then we started the walk of two miles to Tulchan Lodge. Two old boys who are on farms in the neighbourhood, John Edwards and Ernest Bailey met us on the road. We called at the farm where we were getting our potatoes and at the keeper's cottage we saw Mrs Green, who has kindly undertaken to do what cooking was required.

At length we reached our quarters at Tulchan Lodge, a more lovely and ideal spot could not have been found: we were on the edge of a spacious wood, the beautiful Spey below us and miles of moorland rising up behind us. The weather was gloriously fine and the days rushed by all too quickly.

Immediately after breakfast we gathered under a tree and said Matins, and then went off, armed with sacks and a barrow, to some marshy land to gather moss. We were new to the work and the best moss required some looking for, and there were so many distractions, spiders, dragon flies, beetles, frogs, butterflies, ant-hills and wild flowers and we could not help looking at and for them. We returned always to Tulchan for dinner with the appetites of hunters but the pangs were soon fully appeased. Then came the afternoons devoted to pleasure when we scattered where we liked. We shall never forget it all; in years to come our minds will hark back to those days and the happy memories will perhaps cheer gloomy hours when we are immersed in the dreary drudgery of smoky towns. Little "Luke" was there and nobody enjoyed the outing more than he did!"

September 1918

1st

The Warden returned today from Braemar where he preached twice yesterday and where he received much kindness from the Bishop of Aberdeen and Orkney and other friends. The exact sum from the collection is not yet known but will be better than last year.

Attacks on the Germans by Canadian troops forced the Germans to consider withdrawing to the Hindenberg line from where they had launched their offensive in the previous March.

British troops suffered from a lack of reserves and attacks were ceased bringing to an end the Amiens offensive. British and French had 42,000 casualties with the Germans having 100,000 losses and 30,000 troops taken prisoner.

9th

A most handsome gift of £100 has been sent by Mr Howard Morley. Mr Morley was in Braemar Church last Sunday. We cannot sufficiently express our thanks for this very generous gift. Our bank balance was very low and this will help us splendidly to meet our heavy bills this month.

10th

We return sincere thanks to His Grace the Duke of Richmond and Gordon for another fine haunch of venison; and to Mrs Johnstone for a splendid roll of beaver cloth.

The Rev W Tuke has kindly sent £2 towards the Forfar Bed. We are truly sorry to learn that he is leaving Scotland shortly. He has been a very loyal and constant friend for many years and has interested many congregations in the work of the Orphanage.

From Private James Roy Adams

Just a note to say that I am in the best of health and enjoying life out in "No Man's Land" We have had very bad weather lately, but I am glad to tell you it has now quite changed and I hope it will continue.

Well, sir, I was lucky at the base this time before the medical board owing to my arm being disabled, so I got placed in Category B2. I was sorry leaving the old regiment, and I had to part with the Highland dress. We have very nice officers here, so it is not too bad.

I am on the regimental police and have a very nice time of it, but it is not so pleasant when on night duty and the shells are bursting a few yards from you. But it does not matter very much, as I am always saying there are better days coming.

Can you tell me what regiment Colour Sergeant Allan belongs to as I always find his name in the magazine?

The reason I am asking is that we had a Colour-Sergeant M Allan in the 3rd Cameron Highlanders so I am wondering if it is he. I would be very much obliged if you could send on the magazine to me as I am always interested in the Orphanage, or a book of some sort, I am sorry to say there is nothing here we can get because every place is shattered to pieces by the Huns' last offensive. There is not a living soul to be seen except soldiers camped all over the place.

Our company is working on the railway line; that has also been wrecked. I am sending a PO as I promised; I hope you will get it all right. Please tell Mr White I was asking kindly about him and hope he is well. I will send some more soon. With all good wishes, James

11th

The children have been keeping festival today by way of compensation for not being able to go to Lossiemouth. Last evening they had a high tea, which was much enjoyed, the bakers having made great efforts to supply our wants. This afternoon they had a half holiday and went to an entertainment given by a troupe of pierrettes from Cullen, which was a novelty and quite excellent.

The war news has been so encouraging of late that we are beginning to hope that next year it may be "Lossie again"!!

12th

Mrs Laing having heard that we badly need a wheel-chair for a cripple boy has generously sent £10 to provide one. This will be a great boon, very much appreciated and we heartily thank the donor.

American and French forces attacked St Mihiel, south of Verdun which had been continuously held by the Germans since 1914. Despite thick fog and nine German Divisions in opposition, the German resistance collapsed on the first day.

17th

We have received 5s from Sidney Cooper for the Former Inmates' Bed. We are glad to know he is doing well and thriving.

In Turkey, Turkish forces occupied Baku - a significant oil producing centre and the British Force was commanded to withdraw.

Battle of Megiddo started with the British forces led by General Allenby, supported by air power and the Desert Mounted troops made significant gains and Turkish troops were routed and withdrew leaving the British to advance to Damascus and beyond.

20th

We are grateful to Dora Jones for 2s for the Former Inmates' Bed.

25th

Miss Bruce Gardyne has sent us a cheque for £10 for the purpose of starting an endowment of a bed to be called the Battleship Bed in honour of our navy and its good work for us. This is a brilliant idea which we hope will be taken up warmly.

US General Pershing with one million men was holding the front near Argonne, advances were slowed by strong German defences but by early October two of the three German defensive lines had been taken.

British and French troops meanwhile crossed the Canal du Nord and occupied Cambrai within 3 days.

Other armed British Divisions joined the offensive and forced the retreat of further German Forces.

At the end of September, Bulgaria agreed to an Armistice, the first of the Central Powers to do so.

October 1918

1st

We are most grateful to Mr F.A. Hardy, Edinburgh for his kind subscription of two guineas.

The British Forces under General Allenbury entered Damascus, taking 20,000 Turkish prisoners. Arab Guerilla forces had reached Damascus before the British and the Arabs took charge of the city. Beruit and Aleppo were taken by the British within days. French Naval Forces occupied Beruit as a base.

2nd

Many thanks to the children of St John's the Evangelist, Inverness, for their welcome offering of £1 4s 3d, and also to Andrew and Joan Rhodes, Inverness, for a very nice parcel of books and toys for the children.

3rd

A blank day *(This meant no money coming in!!)*

The German chancellor approached the US President Woodrow Wilson and asked for an Armistice on similar lines to the previous one. His request was rejected until their military leadership had been removed.

5th

We received a fine stag from His Grace the Duke of Richmond and Gordon and a grand parcel of garments for the children from J.A.H. and we are most grateful to both.

7th

We are grieved to learn that another of our old boys, David Ramsay, has died of wounds received during the war; he had been eight months in the firing line. R.I.P.

10th

Many thanks to F.H. from Harrogate, for £5 for the Yorkshire Bed. The Warden remembers a conversation at Braemar and he thinks he knows the anonymous donor and is very grateful.

11th

We return best thanks to Viscount Wimbourne for a nice present of venison.

14th

We today received two splendid bales of garments from Miss Macdonald and the Aberlour Orphanage Guild and there is still a parcel to come from the Carnoustie Branch. Once more we tender our sincerest thanks for the invaluable help rendered so constantly by this Guild.

US and French Offensive Meuse Argonne commenced. Initially intense German resistance but soon reinforcements were desperately needed as all sides had suffered heavy losses.

17th

A most valuable parcel of beautiful woollen garments has come from two friends in St Andrews. It is a costly gift and one that is fully appreciated. There will be a great run on the jerseys!

On the western front British forces took 20,000 German troops as prisoners. Fierce fighting in Italy with British troops involved – bridgeheads at Piave were secured by the Anglo- French forces.

(December Magazine records the death of an old boy Samuel Burton at this battle)

22nd

A very good friend has sent us a valuable cheque for £20, half for coals and half for the general fund. We are sincerely grateful for this generous help.

From Private Bertie Bartell

I received the magazine yesterday. It was very good of you to send it. I greatly enjoy reading it.

I am back in the fighting line again, after having a bit of a rest. It is very hot where I am, and Fritz puts up a good fight before he retires. He can do nothing against our artillery, thank God for that. You have no idea what the sound of the guns is like. It is a hundred times louder than thunder. It is good for us to have the Germans out of their well-made dug-outs.

I and some of my pals were in one the other day. We counted 160 steps before we got to the bottom of it. Then we had a fierce hand to hand fight with our bayonets. There were nine of us, and I was the lucky one, as I had a Mills bomb with me. I drew the pin and threw it amongst the six, killing four. We took the other two prisoners. They were glad to come along with us, and we got some useful information out of them. We went to another dug-out and came across a German tin of pork and beans, two loaves and a tin of coffee. We sat down at a table and partook of a good meal. It was the best of enjoyment but it soon came to an end, and we had to be up and out again to chase the enemy. Kindly remember me to all at the Old Home, also Mr White, Mr Symons and Mr Robinson.

23rd

We are most grateful to Mrs Don of South Kensington for £5 towards the Black Watch Bed in memory of her son who belonged to the 1st Battalion, and who was killed on September 14th 1914 and we tender our sincere sympathy.

British forces under General Cobbe advanced from Baghdad and met stiff Turkish resistance. Two days of fighting saw the surrender of the Turks and General Cobbe advanced to Mosul.

25th

We have also a nice parcel of socks and stockings from Miss Montgomery and the Dunkeld and Birnam Stocking Guild, which is a most acceptable gift.

26th

We sincerely thank the children of St Mary's Cathedral, Edinburgh for 17s contributed by them.

CHRISTMAS

Christmas will soon be here. It is a daily topic of conversation amongst our young folks. They are wondering whether, owing to the excessive price of currants and raisins, they will be able to have any pudding this year. We have told them that if they do, the raisins will be so scarce that one will say to the other, "Brother, where art thou?" We are expecting many of our old boys to dinner on Christmas Day, including some of our soldier lads. We fervently hope that peace may reign upon this weary earth ere the Christmas Bells ring out their joyful message.

A HEAVY EXPENSE

We very much regret to say that we have been saddled with the serious task of having to get some of the corridor roofs repaired in fact re-covered. It is impossible to keep them water tight and every shower of rain or snowfall gives us a flood. There is nothing for it but for all the faulty roofs to be thoroughly recoated and it will cost £222. Who will help us foot the bill?

November 1918

VICTORY

For long we have been hoping for peace, and now that it has come the thought of it is almost lost in the joy of Victory; great, glorious and complete victory; more crushing than we had almost dared to hope for!

And now we are looking forward to a Merry Christmas; older hearts will have shadows, but ours are young and shadows never linger with us. We know our friends will remember us, and we shall not forget them.

1st All Saints Day

This is a holiday as usual, and has been much enjoyed in spite of a wet afternoon which prevented a football match. We hope that the next holiday, Founder's Day on December 11th will find the world at peace.

Third stage of the US led offensive to drive forward to the North of France. German resistance was collapsing and US troops moved swiftly along the Meuse River. The offensive ended with the signing of the Armistice.

2nd

We are grieved to hear of another old boy being killed, namely David Thomson; we recorded some time ago he had been awarded the Military Medal, and now we are told that he had received a bar to it three days before he was killed. R.I.P.

4th

Many thanks to the Hon Mrs Muirhead for a welcome donation of £1 16s for a ton of coals.

There was a high cost for the US with 117,000 troops posted as casualties since September.

Middle East- Despite Armistice having been signed with Turkey, General Cobbe was ordered to march into Mosul where the Turks had a garrison. Turkish commander agreed to abandon the town to the British mid-month. Occupation of Mosul signalled the end of the Middle East campaign.

From Private George Partridge, Egyptian Force

I have much pleasure in writing you a few lines just to let you know how I am always getting on. I daresay you will be wondering what has come over me, but I have never forgotten you all. I hope you received my PC letting you know I have been wounded, which I sent about three weeks ago.

I was in the 17th General Hospital in Alexandria for over a fortnight but am now in a convalescent Home, and I must say I like it much better, as we have lots of freedom, and there is everything here you could wish for, such as rowing, yachting and all sorts of amusements.

It is a very lovely spot. One enjoys walking round the grounds. It is a real pleasure to be in such a quiet place after the summer on the firing line.

I got wounded the first day of our advance, 19th September so I did not get very far. I got hit by shrapnel in the leg. My wounds are healing up but I am still a little cripple yet, and cannot go about much without the aid of a stick.

One thing, our wounds have not been in vain. I reckon it was a good piece of work, and I am sure when they got news of it in England there would have been great rejoicing. It seemed to have been the beginning of the end. We are all anxiously looking forward for the end, and let us hope it will not be long, for I am sure all are tired of hearing wars and rumours of wars. I do not expect we will be back for next Christmas yet. I would just like to spend another Christmas with you, for those were happy days. However, I trust to see the Old Home again before I go abroad to settle.

You will be surprised to hear I met W Rattray before I left my regiment, and I assure you he was looking well. We spent a fine evening together and had the usual chat of bygone days. I have also met another old friend, Tom Harris. He is in the same Battalion, but I never have the opportunity to speak to him.

It is a long time since I had a letter from you, Sir, but I daresay you cannot remember everyone, for I know there is plenty of writing to do in your position and it must be very tiring, so we can excuse you. However I hope you will find a few minutes to drop me a line.

I hear from our old friend Mrs Pattison quite regularly, and must say she is a very good correspondent and I do love to read her letters. That is what we boys look for and what cheers us up are letters from home. It is the one and only thing that brightens us up, and if we do not get letters life is very miserable for us.

I have not heard from my brother Ernest since leaving my Battalion, but trust he is still getting on well, also Fred.

What kind of weather are you having in Scotland? I suppose it will be pretty cold. We are having the best of weather here and lovely sunshine. Kindly remember me to all old friends.

French and German Generals met on 7th November and discussed terms for an Armistice which had conditions for the evacuation of German troops from French areas.

British forces were close to occupying Ghent and Mons. Kaiser abdicated and fled to the Netherlands.

11th

Victory at last! Laus Deo!

12th

Very many thanks to Mrs Clutterbuck, Putteridge Bay for £10 towards coals.

15th

A very welcome gift of £10 for Christmas has come from some good friends in Edinburgh, for which we return many thanks. It will be a great help towards "A Merry Christmas".

18th

Mrs Carmichael, Pitlochry, has most kindly sent £5 towards the Black Watch Bed, as a thank offering for the preservation of her husband, Major Carmichael, through two and a half years active service and many hardships with that famous regiment.

We return sincere thanks to Mrs Robberds for £1 "for anything you like" and an order for tulip bulbs. We have made £17 by our tulip bulbs.

Sir George MacPherson Grant has sent us a valuable gift indeed, nothing less than a truck of coal! It can be imagined what this means to us in these days and we cannot adequately express our gratitude.

19th

Our hearts were gladdened on the arrival of a cheque for £20 from the Misses

Chisholm, Beauly, being £10 for coals and £10 for the support of a bed.

We were grieved to receive the following letter from a Chaplain of His Majesty's Forces in Italy.

"It is with deep regret that I send you the sad news that Samuel Burton fell in action on October 27th. He was with his company in that magnificent and most successful crossing and battle of the Piave, and had almost reached the first objective, a bank well guarded by machine guns and snipers when he was shot through the heart. Death was instantaneous. He with two others were buried near where they fell by comrades in another regiment. I found the place that same day and put up a mark-Nuova Casa- is the name of the house opposite. He gave his life in a great cause, and already enjoys his reward. The officers and men in the Battalion join me in sending their deep and heartfelt sympathy. R.I.P."

Sea War - General Beatty accepted the surrender of the German High Seas Fleet.

21st

We have received two handsome "Victory offerings" on behalf of the Endowment Fund for the Yorkshire Bed. There is only a small balance required to complete the £350. We heartily congratulate Miss Fowler Jones on the success of her efforts.

24th

We have gratefully received a donation for Christmas, being "Christopher's birthday present". It is an offering in memory of a gallant young soldier who fell at Bullecourt.

27th

Miss Ferne very kindly sends 10s for coals and 10s "to help to mend the roofs" very welcome!

29th

We are very grateful to Lady Ogilvie Dalgleish for two nice hinds, a valuable present indeed in these days.

30th

Our best wishes to Mr and Mrs Peter Banks (Jeannie Maclennan), old boy and girl, who paid us a visit this week on their honeymoon.

December 1918

Across all the theatres of war, fighting ceased and new states were formed.

The US President travelled to Europe to lead the peace treaties that ended WW1, based on his earlier 14 point Peace programme.

When WW1 ended the scale of destruction and loss of life was unparalleled in human history.

The fighting had lasted from August 1914 to November 1918 with scarcely a day without military activity.

Of 65 million troops mobilised around 8 million were killed and 21 million wounded.

For the British Forces from across the Empire, 8.6 million were mobilised and 908,000 died.

The fighting left severe physical and mental scars on many, impacting on their family, work and whole life.

1st

Many thanks to Lord Wimbourne for a valuable present of venison; and to members of St Mary's Magdalene, Dundee, for an excellent parcel of garments.

3rd

Mr Mc Corquodale sends his usual generous gift of £10 towards Christmas festivities. We hope to have a very bright time this year.

5th

The Provost of Inverness Cathedral sends a goodly sum of £9 from the Cathedral Catechism. We are most grateful for this generous help.

7th

Miss Begbie has again sent a splendid box of chocolate wherewith to celebrate the anniversary of our Founder's birth on December 11th. This will be a great treat, for chocolate is a luxury almost unknown here in these days.

9th

A good friend in Edinburgh sends £10 for Christmas and says "The prospect of peace must make this Christmas happy though it will be sad for many of us."

11th

This is Founder's Day and the 88th anniversary of his birth. It has been observed in the Orphanage as a holiday as usual and has also been marked by the endowment of a bed by an old friend of his and ours.

We have to thank Miss Sharp, Broughty Ferry, for £1 to help our soldier lads to keep Christmas and Private John Tyson for his welcome contribution.

13th

We are very pleased to hear again from Amy Hadrell- Old Girl- who very kindly sends us 7s 6d, of which 5s is for Christmas.

16th

The Rev Sydenham Lindsay has again sent us a welcome contribution from Montreal in the form of $25, which he wishes to go to the Endowment of the Clan Ross bed in memory of Reginald Ivan Ross, parish priest of Ursula Falls.

Miss Stavert very kindly sends £1 from herself and £1 10s from the boys of her Bible Class for Christmas. The Warden lately had the privilege of seeing the King and Queen and the Prince of Wales during their drive through Edinburgh, from the window of the room in which the Bible Class is held. Very many thanks.

18th

Our friends are very good at remembering the children in view of Christmas – listed in two days were no less than 18 donations for funds.

We have received from Mrs Sharp, Balmuir, a roll of over fifty yards of grey flannel, the very thing we wanted and needed badly.

20th

Mr H.A. Baily, Brighton, realizing that we shall have a large party at Christmas, and that, with food at its present price, it will be an expensive business, most kindly sends us a cheque for £5.

Another handsome gift is an anonymous donation of £20, which, at the suggestion of the donor, has been allocated towards the repairs to the roof.

23rd

We have very gratefully received the sum of 14s 3d from the infants of St Martin's Mission Church Sunday School, Dundee. It is very nice of these little people to remember us.

24th

Little Mary Grant, Glen Grant, has again sent a magnificent present of Christmas Crackers, which will give immense delight tomorrow afternoon to everyone. Few things would be missed at Christmas more than crackers if they could not be had.

25th

Christmas Day

This is no holiday for the postman! Our letter bag was almost bursting. Most of the contents were Christmas greetings for the children and staff. But the Orphanage itself had a share of the good things. For example, Captain R Steuart Menzies sent £15, £10 10s from Mr and Mrs Hugh Moncrieff.

Other good gifts are 3 footballs from Mr Morrison, Aberlour.

For all these good things we are most grateful indeed.

26th

Robert Jack has sent 5s for the Former Inmates' Bed, and his brother Matthew adds a message that he has now been discharged from the army and is a coalminer. We hope he will be able to send a lot of much needed coal to the surface!

28th

Mrs Outhwaite has sent us £10 1s 7d, being the Christmas Day Offering in St Michael's Church in Earlsferry. This is very much more than last year, and we are proportionately grateful!

31st

The Warden sincerely thanks all those kind friends who have sent contributions during the past two days and assures them that they are much valued; but he has been so busy with correspondence and household duties that he has not had time to mention them individually before despatching the magazine copy to the printers!

CHRISTMAS DAY

Another Christmas Festival has come and gone. From far and near came expressions of sincere wishes that this first peace Christmas might be a very bright one indeed for the children; not only wishes, but material gifts to help to make it so.

The first day or two of the holidays, before Christmas Day, were bright and frosty, and there was plenty of opportunity for skating and sliding. Christmas Day was not so good for this sport but there were other attractions then and the frost returned soon after.

The scarcity of paper, including coloured tissue paper, again prevented the manufacture of chains and other decorations of that kind, but many children had been most diligent in painting mottoes and sketches, and these, together with the decorations that had been carefully preserved from former years gave the place a very festive appearance. We congratulate and thank the young artists.

At 3.30 on Christmas Eve the usual peregrinations from room to room to examine the decorations took place and comment, praise and comparisons were plentiful. At 5 o'clock we went to Church and sang the first Evensong of Christmas. After tea the rest of the evening was spent in the more prosaic duties of boot cleaning and other domestic arrangements for the next day.

On Christmas morning we were early awake and some were early astir; kitchen fires had to be alight by 4 o'clock and by 6 o'clock life began to be general. A goodly number made their communion at 7 o'clock and others at 8 o'clock. At 10 o'clock there was a short service for the little ones and at half past 11 a Choral Eucharist for all the others.

Then came dinner. Christmas dinner, when currants, raisins and apples are not to be had, must be a sore anxiety to those who have to arrange for it (we got 1lb of currants for 570 people!) But the feasters had no anxiety and no disappointment. The dinner was quite excellent, and called for great praise to those who provided it. What the Christmas pudding was made of we cannot say, but there it was! Or rather we should say there they were, for we were told that no less than 50 puddings had been made! We all did justice to the good fare, and afterwards cheered and shouted ourselves hoarse. Ten old boys, three in uniform, one of whom had been wounded, sat down to dinner and two "old girls", both now the wives of "old boys". We hope that next year there will be many more returned soldiers with us to share the feast. For an hour or so after dinner we exercised to make room for tea. Tea-time provided as usual one of the great attractions and pleasures of Christmastide, namely crackers: many of them contained musical (?!!) instruments of which we had full benefit for a day or two.

Then at night came the dance. We kept it up till half past eleven. The music was excellent and the dancing first-rate. We would admit we were tired when we fell in round the big dining hall to sing Auld Lang Syne, but it was observed that we soon went to sleep and were rather quiet the next morning.

Then on New Year's Eve, we danced again till a bell told us that the New Year had begun, and that Christmas was almost over once more. This time next year many of us will be far away and looking back with fond memories to the fun that can never return, as many who were with us last year are doing now.

Most sincerely we thank all those who contributed in any way, by gifts, services or good temper, towards the great happiness of our Christmas and we wish them all

A BRIGHT AND HAPPY NEW YEAR!

Although the letters from old boys reduced in number after the War ended, several of the old boys were still in the Army and Navy and continued to correspond with the Orphanage.

Other letters like the following gave news of the deaths of old boys.

In the summer of 1919, a letter was published in the Journal about Sergeant John Anderson

The following letter was the last received by a lady who had befriended the writer - the late *Sergeant John Anderson, Gordon Highlanders*. He joined the regular army as a lad. When he presented himself for enlistment he was rejected, owing to the malformation of one of his toes. The Authorities informed him that he would be obliged to undergo an operation. This he immediately did. His great ambition when a boy was to win the Victoria Cross. He fell, gallantly leading his men, at the Battle of Loos.

[He died on 13th October 1915 when 62,000 British troops perished as well as 26,000 German soldiers.]

"Dear Madam,

This is an acknowledgement of your very generous and delightful parcel, which I received just as I returned from the trenches. It was a most agreeable surprise to me. Everything was of the most suitable nature, just what was required. It seems as though you must have known exactly our needs. I am most grateful to you. I can only return my sincerest thanks for your splendid gifts. How can we do anything else but fight with a good heart, when we have such splendid folks as you at home to remember us out here.

It is such remembrances that made the British soldier what he is, of cheery disposition, and ready to surmount any obstacle which comes in his way. The thought of Home, Sweet Home, and friends at home, who never forget the Boys at the Front are incentive enough for any man I should think. And we fully appreciate the kindnesses that are showered upon us by our friends at home.

Well I am sorry that I must close now, as time is short, but in doing so let me once more tender my sincerest thanks to you and yours, and hope you may long be spared to enjoy life at its best. I remain, yours faithfully, J ANDERSON"

1919 saw a return to more normal conditions in the Orphanage with the diary entries relating to finance and the still increasing costs of basic necessities. A few of the letters received into 1919 are transcribed below.

January 1919

From Private Ernest Bannerman - Gordon Highlanders

Just a short note hoping this finds you in the best of health. Well, sir, you will see by the above (Address) that I am not with my original unit, but was transferred to a Prisoner of War Company where I am at present escorting German Prisoners of War. It is not a bad job, but we are out in a lonely spot away up in the wilds of France, miles from any village or town, so you can see we spent a very quiet Christmas.

We had mashed potatoes, beans and half a pound of plum pudding for dinner, and then we had two or three packets of cigarettes, and there were a few presents of writing pads which were presented by the Captain. He played the gramophone during the dinner hour. We spent a happy day.

I expect you had a very jolly Xmas as there was no fighting going on as in the past four years. Were there many soldiers over? I hope it will not be too long ere we are all home again.

There is nothing but wrecked houses and barbed wire and shells lying round the place. We are having very rough weather, nothing but wind and rain.

I wish you all a Happy New Year.

In the February Magazine there is a report of the experiences of one old boy Thomas Laycock. It appeared in the Penrith Observer, it was headed "Comrade beaten to death by the Germans".

"Private Thomas Laycock was taken prisoner at Chemin de Dames between Soissons and Rheims on May 27th 1918. He was attached to a Royal Engineer's working party, and, following an intense enemy bombardment, he was one of the party obliged to surrender. The Germans immediately took all their effects, and even appropriated their rations. The men were set to work repairing the road about two miles behind the lines, and for the first five days they were served no food.

One night they ascertained that soup was being prepared for them, and in their eagerness to break their long fast they rushed in a body, but the famishing men were not only driven back at bayonet's point but denied any share of the soup.

Two prisoners some weeks later escaped during night time but at Namur they were captured and beaten with sticks and given only bread and water for several days. Their boots were taken and they were given a pair of rough clogs. One prisoner was beaten to death by the guards for having drunk some liquor from bottles they were moving from one place to another.

When it was evident that the war was drawing to a close in November, the guards no longer kept a close watch and on the night of 9th to 10th November, Laycock and two other men left the camp and made off in the direction of the Allies' line.

The wanderers struck the American lines on Tuesday 12th November, the day following the Armistice and were given a rousing welcome. While Laycock was a prisoner, the French civilian population befriended them whenever possible, and often passed bread to them through the cage wire. Although many were sent, Laycock never received a letter or parcel while he was a prisoner."

Two letters which stood out with a lot of interesting information are transcribed below

From Alexander Sprenger in March and April 1919

Yesterday I had official confirmation to the effect that since the termination of the war, letter censoring had been abolished. Such being the case, I hasten to write you as long a letter as I can.

Alexander describes his wartime experiences that take him from Southampton to Beirut via France, Italy and Malta.

I left Southampton and sailed for Cherbourg in France, the voyage being a little over twenty four hours... On our arrival at Cherbourg we walked five miles to an American rest camp. We were very tired and fatigued... We continued our journey next day in a passenger train (cattle trucks) and had a run through to St Germains. During this journey we had about fifty stops. We used to get the engine driver to halt near vineyards, and then jump out and pick the grapes. Any fruit came under our closest observation, and we did full justice to it, since our rations were very small.

We were rather late in arriving at St. Germains, the consequence being we had little or no time there – only a night,,, There were exactly in our truck forty men. We had only a blanket and waterproof sheet. Some slept on the floor packed like sardines, and some slept on seats provided for the journey. I had a seat, which was the best choice of the two and my bones were sore every morning when I woke up... To crown it all our cigarettes and tobacco gave out, and we would have willingly smoked tea leaves had there been any to smoke...

Every day we stopped at an appointed place for a cup of hot tea. It was the only liquid we had on our journey, with the exception of water, which was also scarce. While on the border station between France and Italy a woman sold us some large apples, and it was the first real feed I had up to then... We passed through the Riviera, and oh! It was a lovely sight... Mile after mile of gorgeous blue lake, mile after mile of mountain ridges with their snow capped peaks, and mile after mile of greenery on the banks of the lakes... ...It has been without a doubt the most beautiful and wonderful scene of my life. I think one could travel far and fail to find such loveliness...

...We journeyed on to Toranto and ran short of water. We were absolutely gasping for a drink. We took no precautions against a shortage and the consequence was that we ran short, and could not get any until we reached our last rest camp at a place called Cimone. That was a rotten place too. Gee whiz, I was glad to get out of it. I was there for about three days and each evening prior to tea we had a dose of quinine. Lovely sweet tasting stuff, I can assure you – ugh! I can feel the taste in my mouth yet.

Latterly we sailed to Malta. We arrived in Malta about thirty six hours after our departure from Cimone. Malta is to me a lovely spot, but I hear contrary opinions on all sides. It is reckoned to be one of the greatest fever beds in the world...

...I stayed two nights and a day in Malta, but we telegraphists were very scarce and needed at Port Said. They had to send some of us there and some to Madras. I got along with my chums to Port Said and whilst there went through a Morse examination for a land station. I came out top and was put down with another O.T. and a telegraphist... Then there came a letter to relieve a sick man... when I came here it was only after the Turks had evacuated it seven days previously... I am at a place called Beirut... it is the biggest seaport town in Palestine... Life out here is not so bad, but fever and the flu are the white man's enemy. More men have been lost with malaria than have died on the battlefield...

...Rumours are prevalent that it will not be long before we are home... We have nearly finished the minesweeping and I expect it will not be long before it is all done... Needless to say there are plenty other things I could speak about but they escape my memory for the moment. I will tell you lots of things when I get home to 'Blighty'. In the meantime I will "pipe down" as the Navy calls it!

May 1919

Letter from an old boy

From Private Percy Hay (Tank Corps)

I am very sorry I seldom write, but I can never forget the dear old Home. I expected to have been over on leave but no luck yet. I was sent up here to escort two prisoners, who are to be tried by court martial in Cologne, so I am not here for the army of occupation yet, but I expect coming up to some part of Germany after I join my battalion in France.

It is a beautiful city, and there is a handsome cathedral, and I wonder what the Germans would say if we had bombed it in the same way as they did to churches in Belguim and France. We have plenty of amusements, and some nice swimming baths to go to. I wonder if any of the old boys are up here because I would be very glad to have a talk to them about the old days. I often wonder if Mrs Veitch is still at the Home, as I will never forget her, as she nursed me when I was very ill, at Christmas 1912.

I have just been to Church, but it is nothing like the nice services at Aberlour, and I am afraid I have no voice to be in a choir now.

Please remember me to Mr White and all who know me. Hoping you are all keeping in the best of health.

One event relating to the recent peace was included for 19ᵗʰ July 1919

Our children took part today in the Parish Peace Celebrations, and had a great time in Aberlour House grounds and at the bonfire at night. Several of the boys managed to snatch pieces of the flag which was hoisted on the pole in the middle of the fire; the pole fell before the flag was burnt, and there was a scramble for the trophy. The boys are going to preserve the pieces to show to their grandchildren in years to come!!

The July 1919 Magazine reported the Annual General Meeting and some extracts are included below.

Manager's report July 1919

We rejoice that the cessation of hostilities put a stop to the growth of that long list of old boys who have lain down their lives in defence of the Empire and we rejoice that their sacrifice has proved not in vain. Our list includes 60 names but we feel sure that it is by no means complete, and we are taking steps to gather in as many as possible of other names that should be included in it.

We feel that a worthy memorial should be raised to these brave lads and a few months ago we put forward a suggestion as to the form it should take. It was to be in the nature of a comfortable hostel for the use of old boys and other uses when not in use as a hostel. We estimated that about £1000 would be needed. The scheme has not met with the support we anticipated and unless contributions come in more rapidly we must either modify the plan or find some other means of providing the money.

(The question of a War Memorial was discussed many times in subsequent magazines).

We resumed possession of our Isolation Hospital in the spring and received sincere expressions of gratitude from the VAD for its use during the war. Some 500 soldiers had been located there and it was handed back to us in every bit as good a condition as when we handed it over.

At the beginning of the war it seemed as if evil days must come upon us at once, and yet at the end of it has found us with largely increased endowments, a credit revenue balance and no debts. We thank God and take courage.

Postscript

The final postscript to these letters and journals comes from the Magazine of June 1920 where the Warden records

"There would be a Churchyard Cross designed we hope to be worthy of those who gave their lives for us"

This simple cross remains a memorial to those old boys who never came back to the only home they knew.

As readers will see many of the names on this simple granite cross dedicated in 1929 were regular letter writers to Aberlour during WW1

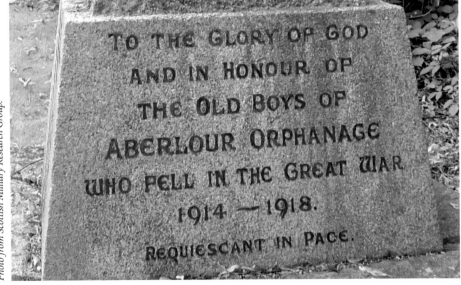

Photo from Scottish Military Research Group.

DAVID ABERDEIN
JOHN ANDERSON
ANDERSON AUCHTERLONIE
ALEXANDER BAIN
ARCHIBALD BAKER
WILLIAM BALD
JOHN BANKS
ALBERT BARTELL
JOHN BLACK
ALEXANDER BAXTER
JAMES BOYD
ALEXANDER BROWN
DANIEL BROWN
ROBERT BROWN
SAMUEL BURTON
JAMES COOK

Photo from Scottish Military Research Group.

FREDERICK DAZLEY
ALFRED DINNIE
DAVID DOUGLAS
HARRY DOUGLAS
PATRICK DUFF
ROBERT DUNBAR
JAMES DUNCAN
JOHN DURRANT
JAMES GARDEN
JOHN GARDNER
WALTER GEDDES
WILLIAM GOURLAY
ROBERT GRANT
ALEXANDER GRAY
PATRICK HAMILTON
HENRY HANDFORTH

Photo from Scottish Military Research Group.

Photo from Scottish Military Research Group.

Some did return and did not forget Aberlour and their days there.

One who survived for many years after the War was Ben Pritchard.

Ben Pritchard came to Aberlour in June 1900 as a boy of 7. He was born in the South of England and was living in Twyford before being admitted to Aberlour Orphanage.

Like many of the children who came to Aberlour in the late 1890s Ben was probably referred by a clergyman in his home village.

Ben left Aberlour in August 1908 for Fort William.

He served in the 1st Seaforths during WW1 where he found his vocation as a medical attendant in field hospitals and was seen as compassionate and caring to all injured soldiers.

His love of flowers, developed by his contact with Mr White from the Orphanage, was evident from his letters home to Aberlour.

When he returned to England after the war his work often involved gardening and parks. He spent time in New Zealand and designed public parks there.

When he was 92 he was featured in a local North of England paper as going back to school, to teach horticulture to some secondary school children. Ben lived some years after that and I was delighted to meet his great grandson on a visit to Scotland. He and his family were very pleased to see Ben recognised and valued in this book.

Another survivor was Arthur Mylam who wrote such wonderful descriptive letters during WW1.

Arthur was born in the Marylebone Workhouse in December 1890. He came to Aberlour in 1897 but it is not clear where he was living till then. No contact with his mother was recorded. Arthur was an acute observer of the world and of the people from the different places he was posted. After the war Arthur worked on the Railways, he was married to Violet Painton in 1924 and had two children Arthur and Lilian. Arthur died aged 64.

His son, also Arthur, was a poet.

Arthur senior clearly passed on to his son his questions about war, the suffering and the futility of conflict. His son's poem about Remembrance Day seems a fitting way to close this collection of Aberlour memories.

Remembrance Day

The cold November wind blows leaves and old remembering men down the canyon of Whitehall

Ben's Salome bell the world to silence calls. 'Til distant guns, echoes of another time, take up the dirge

Old men with tearful eyes stride by with scarlet wreath.

In many a town and village, around the granite cross are gathered ageing mourners, remembering their loss.

And did those other Whitehall men feel no guilt or shame to send young men in thousands out to kill and to be maimed?

Like lemmings they went forth to clear the cliffs of death, and with them took another nation's sons

Yet still the madness is not cured, though all the faiths agree, we do not heed God's command. Thou shalt not kill for me.

Grieve at the going down of the sun and in the morning, remember – But have we learnt oh! Have we learnt, the lessons of November?

By Arthur F Mylam